CISTERCIAN STUDIES SERIES: NUMBER ONE HUNDRED FORTY-SEVEN

The Contemplative Path

Reflections on Recovering a Lost Tradition

The Contemplative Path

Reflections on Recovering a Lost Tradition

E. Rozanne Elder, editor

Cistercian Publications Inc
Kalamazoo, Michigan - Spencer, Massachusetts

The work of Cistercian Publications is made possible in part
by support from Western Michigan University to
The Institute of Cistercian Studies

Available from
Cistercian Publications
Saint Joseph's Abbey
Spencer, Massachusetts 01562

Acknowledgements

Citations from *Luther and the Mystics* by Bengt R.
Hoffman, copyright © Augsburg Publishing House.
Used by permission of Augsburg Fortress Publishers.

Citations from 'A Lamb Goes Uncomplaining Forth'.
Text copyright © 1978 *Lutheran Book of Worship.*
Reprinted by permission of Augsburg Fortress Publishers.

THE CONTEMPLATIVE PATH
Reflections on Recovering a Lost Tradition
ISBN 087907 547 3

Typeset by Photo Composition Service
Printed in the United States of America

TABLE OF CONTENTS

FOREWORD

'Between the body and the mind,' wrote John Cassian in the fifth century, 'there is an inseparable reciprocal connection.'[1] As he described the austere lives of distant desert monks to his gallic contemporaries, he reminded them over and over again that physical austerity was a means to an end, a training exercise for the unceasing awareness of God to which Saint Paul had exhorted all believers when he wrote, 'Always be joyful, pray continually. For everything give thanks, for this is what God in Christ wills for you.'[2]

The papers in this volume represent a small attempt to reach across the gulf by which generations of westerners have divided physical being from cognitive and spiritual being. With a generous grant from The Fetzer Institute, the Institute of Cistercian Studies in August of 1993 brought together a group of teachers, lawyers, housewives, academics, pastors, and monastics to explore together the contemplative tradition within Christianity.

The two sponsoring institutes approached the subject from different starting points. The Institute of Cistercian Studies represents the two quite different disciplinary traditions of cloister

1. Conference 9.2.
2. 1 Thess 5:16–18.

and university. Co-sponsored by Cistercian Publications, a firm specializing in translations of late antique and medieval monastic texts, and by Western Michigan University, a large multi-faceted state institution, the Cistercian Institute encourages research on the monastic tradition within Christianity. Its library holdings of medieval manuscripts and scholarly books on cistercian monasticism, its annual conference at which scholars from across North America and Europe share their research, and—from time to time as funding allows—small workshops exploring themes within that tradition[3] reply on the resources of a small, specialized press and a large state university with many on-going avenues of research.

The Fetzer Institute is a private research foundation dedicated to exploration of the link between the physical world and human consciousness. It is based in science and eclectic in its methodology. Endowed by its founder, broadcaster John Fetzer, the Fetzer Institute sponsors a number of projects which explore the integrity of the human person. Among its many projects is the acclaimed public television series, 'Healing and the Mind with Bill Moyers'.

'New Age' and 'Medieval' Institutes teamed up, convinced from their different starting points that modern persons suffer a fragmentation which divides body from soul and soul from spirit, and that this is unnatural and unhealthy. Contemplatives of all traditions have held this same premise.

The subtitle of the workshop, Rediscovering a Lost Tradition, was chosen to underline the historical fact that, although people today usually identify meditation and receptivity with Far Eastern religions, the contemplative spirit is, in fact, indigenous to the western religious tradition. Over the long, formative

---

3. Previous workshops, co-sponsored by The Medieval Institute of Western Michigan University, resulted in the volumes *The Spirituality of Western Christendom* (1975), *The Roots of the Modern Christian Tradition* (1984), and *From Cloister to Classroom: Monastic and Scholastic Approaches to Truth* (1986).

period of Christianity, the Fathers of the Church consistently taught that effective preaching and social action grow out of sustained prayer. In the early medieval period, while barbarian armies converted to Christianity chiefly to get supernatural power on the side of their armies, it was contemplatives who quietly taught by word and example the deeper meaning of people's new faith. As the centuries passed, activity came to be prized above and apart from prayer, even by Christians. The 'spiritual life' got detached from 'real life'; the soul and the mind were divorced from the body. Until the recent surge of interest in physical fitness, physical discipline had come to be associated only with athletes—a throw back to the pre-Christian meaning of *ascesis*. A theologian has come to be regarded as person of intellectual acuity but not necessarily as a person of physical discipline and of prayer[4]

Each speaker in a different way spoke on prayer, that 'colloquy with God'[5] which lies at the heart of a contemplative life. In what follows therefore there are chapters on liturgical prayer, the public worship in which people use the words of Scripture to respond to the revelation of Scripture; on monologistic, single-word or 'centering' prayer; on the sung prayer of hymnody; and on physical activity as prayer. The integrative theme of the workshop was carried into the daily schedule. Before and after listening to lectures and participating in discussions, members of the workshop had the opportunity of doing yoga exercises under the direction of Mary Stewart, and of sharing daily prayer according to the usages of the

4. See, for comparison, Evagrius Ponticus: 'If you are a theologian you truly pray. If you truly pray you are a theologian'. *Chapters on Prayer*, 60 (*Evagrius Ponticus: The Praktikos and Chapters on Prayer*, translated by John Eudes Bamberger OCSO, Cistercian Studies Series, Number 4 (Spencer-Kalamazoo, 1972) p. 65.

5. Gregory of Nyssa, *On the Lord's Prayer*, 1; Lancelot Andrewes, Points of Meditation Before Prayer, *Preces privatae*, translated F. E. Brightman (London, 1903; New York, 1961).

Benedictines and Cistercians, the Coptic and the Russian Orthodox, the Lutheran and the Anglican churches. They ate vegetarian meals in the beautiful dining room of the Fetzer Institute and slept in ascetic quarters usually occupied by Western Michigan University students. Even the daily ride between the two institutes came to be a paradigm of the passage between two worlds along the contemplative path.

E.R.E.

INTRODUCTION

Robert F. Lehman

W HEN THE FETZER Institute agreed to co-sponsor the workshop that served as the basis for this book, I was asked, 'Why is an organization that funds scientific research to explore the relationship of mind and body in health interested in our monastic traditions?' The specific question for Fetzer is, I believe, part of a larger question of the role of contemplative values in the contemporary society. The papers in this book are a step toward examining that question.

The workshop, held in August 1991, led me on a personal journey that has formed a strong bias. I've come to believe that our modern secular life is in desperate need of reconnecting with its spiritual foundations. The dismal harvest of modern social action should demonstrate, that, no matter how well-intentioned, our public and personal active lives are not planted in fertile soil. Our great spiritual traditions have taught that the contemplative life is not the opposite of the active life, but its true source.

We were also taught in our school history classes that during the Dark Ages the european monasteries were islands preserving for a later age our classical intellectual heritage. As we approach the beginning of a new millennium, we may once again find western civilization turning to the contemplative

traditions. This time, civilization is not in search of its intellect
and mind, but of its heart and soul.

Each of the chapters which follow deals with prayer, the
'colloquy with God' which lies at the heart of a contemplative
life. A liturgist, Paul Bradshaw, explains the ways of common
prayer which developed in the early Christian Church: the
corporate daily worship of Christians together and the solitary
worship which later became the monastic daily office. A New
Testament scholar, John Breck, then guides us to the Eastern
Christian tradition of prayer of the heart, the constant attentiveness to God in silence and solitude known as hesychasm.
A cistercian nun, GilChrist Lavigne, writes of the benedictine
integration of prayer and work (and in the course of the
workshop put us to work to experience it!), and a monk, Basil
Pennington, describes a practical method of prayer which has
been practised by countless generations of monks and nuns
and shared with christian men and women living 'in the world'.
And once out of the cloister, we are taken by Gus Kopka,
Jr, to the world of Pietism, a european protestant expression
of prayer of the heart. Finally, one of the participants, and
the cousin of one of the speakers, Jasper Green Pennington,
reflects on the experience of the workshop and the reflections
which it set off for him.

The ancient contemplative maxim, *actio sequitur esse*, 'action
follows being', needs to become the golden rule of the post-
modern world. The practice of being can no longer be kept
within monastery walls. We need to find ways to integrate
contemplative values into ordinary lives.

TRANSFORMATIVE BEING

Centering Prayer and The Contemplative Path

M. Basil Pennington, ocso

F IRST A WORD of warning. Contemplation must not be seen as a goal, as something to be achieved by us, a state to be attained. God alone is the goal. Union and communion with him is what we want, what we are made for, what he made us for. If we start concentrating on the union, the communion, the contemplation itself, this prevents us from attaining what we seek. Our intent must be wholly on God. This will allow God to bring about the union and communion and the deep, renewing contemplative rest.

A purity of heart is needed here. This is why spiritual teachers and writers have always made so much of asceticism. They saw clearly this need for purity of heart. But here again there is a danger. Asceticism can become the project. Attaining purity of heart can become the goal. And we will again be back to ourselves, seeking something for ourselves, even though in theory we recognize that it is for God to prepare us for union with him.

The matter is subtle. The false self is very sly. It will insinuate itself into anything we undertake. We have to be as wise as serpents and as simple as doves. The simpler, the more clear and direct we are in our pursuit of God, the better chance will we have of avoiding the wiles of the false self which so often undermine the best efforts of the best of us. The simple ancient method of prayer which has come to be called in our time Centering Prayer is a very effective help here, if it is practised with a certain tenacious persistence.

CENTERING PRAYER

Let me describe this way of prayer. I will be rather brief here for I have written a number of books on the subject and Father Thomas Keating has also written on it with masterly insight.

Centering Prayer is a new name for a very ancient form of prayer. Its origins are the same as those of the Jesus Prayer, but in this case it was taught by a westerner, John Cassian. Going in search of a spiritual father, he found one in Abba Isaac, who was reputed to be the holiest, most experienced, and wisest father among the monks in the Egyptian desert at the end of the fourth century. John's quest had been a long one and he was filled with joy when the holy old man taught him how to find contemplative peace. Later John himself became a spiritual father, and a community of men as well as a community of women gathered around him after he moved to the West. For these disciples he undertook to write down what he had learned from the venerated fathers in the desert.[1] A century later another great spiritual father rose up in the West. His name was Benedict, from Nursia in Italy. He wrote a Rule for Monasteries which became very widespread, eventually becoming—for many years—the only monastic rule in the West.[2] In his rule he recommended that his disciples turn to John Cassian's record of the conferences of Abba Isaac

1. The Conferences of John Cassian. English translation in the Nicene and Post-Nicene Fathers series, volume 11.
2. RB 1980 (Collegeville: Liturgical Press).

and others for deep, rich spiritual teaching. So the teaching John received in the desert passed into the mainstream of western spirituality. We find it developed in the earliest spiritual writings we have in English. One in particular, that of an author who humbly hid in anonymity, became very popular and has held its popularity through all the ensuing centuries. His little work, called *The Cloud of Unknowing*,[3] written for one of the father's spiritual sons, is not easy to read because it belongs to a time long past, but its teaching provides much wise counsel. This treatise and many others give witness to how widely this sort of contemplative prayer was practised among ordinary people. It was not the preserve of monks and nuns, though they were the principal teachers. And because they were the teachers, when monasteries were destroyed during the Protestant Reformation and the French Revolution, the practice of this form of prayer was largely lost. Only in our times is it again being widely taught and practised among faithful Christians.

Traditionally this way of prayer has had many names. It is the culmination of *lectio* and so did not need a particular name. It is *contemplatio*. It is prayer in the heart: the mind, the attention come down into the heart and quietly abide there. To achieve this, Abba Isaac counseled Cassian to be content with the poverty of a single simple word. The author of *The Cloud of Unknowing*, pressed this further: Choose a simple word, a single syllable word is best, such as 'God' or 'love'. He added: choose a word that is meaningful to you, the meaning being: 'I am all yours, Lord'. This little word is fixed in the mind. It represents God and only God. It abides there, keeping the mind and heart in God. Anything else that comes

---

3. There are several translations: James Walsh SJ, ed. (New York: Paulist, 1981); Ira Progoff (London: Rider-New York: Julian, 1959); William Johnston, *The Cloud of Unknowing and the Book of Privy Counselling*. NY: Doubleday.

along is simply let go. This little word is our sole response. God is our sole concern during this time of love. It is as simple as that.

The word has power and meaning, for it is the fruit of *lectio*. *Contemplatio* always presupposes *lectio*. All prayer is a response. God speaks to us. We allow his word to come alive in us. It forms us and calls us into ever deeper union. It transforms us until we have the mind and heart of Christ.

To facilitate the teaching and practice of this very traditional prayer form we will set it forth in three simple points, with a bit of a preface and a final word. Let us look at these now.

The preface concerns posture at prayer. Some traditions make more of this than others. This tradition keeps it simple. Sit quietly; that is all the author of *The Cloud of Unknowing* has to say about posture. Sit quietly. That means finding a place where we can expect to be left undisturbed while praying. This may mean putting a note on our door or taking the phone off the hook. Though it is quite possible to sit in a library or an airport (not to mention a church) or some other public place and feel confident that no one will bother us, a quiet place is perhaps more helpful, especially when we are first beginning the prayer and have not developed the facility of letting sounds go by. Sit quietly. Find a good chair. Let the body be settled comfortably. Not too comfortably—or we will soon be snoring. If our back is well supported and relatively straight, the energies can freely flow up and down the spinal system, a part of the refreshment and renewal the prayer affords. We close the eyes gently, fostering the inner quiet, the movement to that place within, the center, where God, the source of our being, dwells.

Sit quietly, the back straight and well supported, the eyes gently closed, in a place where we can expect to be left undisturbed.

Enough for the preface, let us look at the Centering Prayer method itself:

1. *Be in faith and love to God who dwells within.*

Be. Centering is a prayer of being, not of thinking, saying, imagining, feeling, or doing anything. It is simply being to God, with God in love. We do not give God our thoughts, or words, or images, or feelings—we give God our very selves. We simply 'are' to God.

In faith. Faith is the wonderful gift from God by which we *know* that whatever he has said is true, because he can never deceive or be deceived. And he has told us that he will dwell within us. 'The Father and I will come and we will make our dwelling within you.'

And love. Love is gift. I remember a line from a song: Love is not love until it is given away. Love is a give away. We simply give ourselves to God. For these twenty minutes we are all his for him to do with us whatever he wishes. We are willing to let all our own thoughts, ideas, plans, aspirations, and doings go and simply rest with God and let him do whatever he wants with us during this time of love.

To God within. God is everywhere. It is possible to center upon God in others and in other things. Catholics have often enough centered upon our Lord present in the tabernacle. Our Orthodox brothers and sisters often center on God present within the icon. We can center upon the Lord in a the living flame of a candle or in the beauty of a flower or even in a sound, but there is danger here of getting centered in the outward sign and not in the imageless God within. We might choose to center upon the Lord present in the heart of Mary. God is everywhere, but his chosen dwelling, the place where he abides in love with the one whom he loves, is deep within, at the center and ground of our being. Of all the icons this is the best, for we are each the icon God has made of himself, the true icon made in his own image and likeness. God is within. In the Centering Prayer we very simply rest within with him.

This in essence is the whole of the prayer: simply resting with God in love. In order to facilitate our resting there with him we have a second point:

> 2. *We take up a love word and let it be gently present, supporting our being to God in faith-filled love.*

A love word or a prayer word. As we have seen, the Fathers recommend a very simple word, even going so far as to say it should be a single-syllable word. But always remember: Where the Spirit is, there is freedom. Choose what is for you a meaningful word—the meaning being: 'I am all yours, God.' We do not need to repeat this word constantly as one might repeat a mantra. The word is there, a little arrow, pointing us wholly to the Lord, our love. We let it, as it were, gently repeat itself if it will. We rest in God.

Soon enough, alas, if the Lord does not embrace us with a very special love—and he sometimes does—we will discover ourselves off, chasing some thought or memory or feeling or plan or fear. And so we need a third point:

> 3. *Whenever, during the time of our prayer, we become aware of anything, we simply, gently return to the Lord, with the use of our word.*

During the time of the prayer. We usually recommend twenty minutes twice a day. Morning and evening prayer at the cardinal points of the day seems to be universally recommended. What we do know is that those who center twice a day arrive much more quickly at a centered life, a life filled with the fruits of centering: love, joy, peace, patience, kindness, gentleness. The experience of many—and I mean many, thousands upon thousands—recommends twenty minutes. Yet again, where the Spirit is, there is freedom. Experience will lead some individuals to choose a longer or shorter period. And many will choose to have more than two periods a day. In any case, during the time of our prayer we are willing to let God take care of his creation. It is the time for love. We have twenty-three–plus hours to attend to others and their needs and to attend to God himself in the many other wonderful ways in which we can pray and listen to him. Now is the time to rest in love. This time, which the Beloved loves, will give depth and richness to all the other time and all the doings of life.

Whenever we become aware of anything. Good, bad or indifferent, no matter what our mind or imagination, our hearing or our feelings, serve up, our response is ever the same. During this time, as soon as we become aware that our attention is no longer one hundred percent on God, we gently turn back to him with the use of our little word of love. We want to love him with our whole mind, our whole heart, our whole soul, and all our strength.

Simply, gently. No big show about it. Otherwise the fuss itself might take us more away from God than does the intrusive thought or image. Simply: back to God. We do not try to get rid of the thoughts or images. We will never succeed in this. We simply turn to God and, automatically, as we turn to him we turn away from them. We are gentle with ourselves, knowing that we will ever be having thoughts and images and desires and feelings. There is nothing wrong in this. The moment of awareness is the moment of choice. I choose God—gently, using my love word—and again I am centered. Each time I return to the Lord, I choose him again—it is a perfect act of love. He gently asks us: Do you love me more than these? And we answer gently with our word: Yes.

This is the little method passed down through the centuries. Although I have been centering for over forty years and have shared with thousands who have been enjoying the fruits of Centering Prayer in their lives, I am still amazed how such a simple little thing as sitting quietly with the Lord for twenty minutes twice a day can have such a transforming effect. Yet it does.

And the 'final word': At the end of the twenty minutes, let the prayer word go and let the Lord's Prayer (or some other favorite prayer) quietly pray itself within.

We leave the quiet rest of contemplation and enter into a more active prayer as we prepare to enter back into our active lives. Jesus gave us something wonderful in the Lord's Prayer. It is not just a prayer formula, it is a whole school of prayer, a school of life. If we let it gently, unhurriedly unfold within us, it will teach us many things, teach us more and more deeply. During these minutes of quiet emergence, some of the deep things the Lord was teaching us in the silence will come to the surface of our minds to be carried back into life's activity. These two or three minutes can be very rich, so we do not want to hurry them.

Here then is the simple traditional way of entering into contemplative prayer that comes to us through the centuries and is now set forth in a simple, practical 'packaging':

CENTERING PRAYER

Sit quietly, eyes gently closed.
1. *Be in faith and love to God who dwells within.*
2. *Take up a love word and let it be gently present, supporting our being to God in faith-filled love.*
3. *Whenever, during the time of our prayer, we become aware of anything, simply, gently return to the Lord, with the use of our word.*

At the end of the twenty minutes, let the prayer word go and let the Lord's Prayer (or some other favorite prayer) quietly pray itself within you.

THE FRUITS OF CENTERING PRAYER

I hesitate to speak about the fruits of contemplation. Contemplation is in a way a sheer waste. It is Mary, breaking open the costly alabaster jar of fragrant perfume and letting the whole of its costly content gush out on the feet of the Lord. Contemplation is a luxury that the Christian can ill afford. There is so much to be done. Our concern for the poor cries out to us to make better use of our scant time. Yet it is a luxury we can ill afford to do without. Because our Lord wants it, wants it very much. And because, if we do not heed his call, we will not long be able to do anything else of real worth and effectiveness.

Yet if we begin to detail the rich fruits that flow from this little practice of love, there is great danger that we will vitiate the offering; we will begin to seek the fruits and turn our prayer into a project of the false self instead of making it a gift of purest love. If, in fact, we do this, we will frustrate ourselves. For when we begin to seek something for ourselves rather than giving ourselves in purest love to the Lord, we no longer truly center on God and the fruits will no longer be produced.

The false self is made up of what I do, what I have, and what others think of me. (That last one has a real hook in us: what others think of me!) This is the self which Jesus said must die so that our true self can emerge. When we center we really 'kill' the false self. For what are we doing? Just sitting there, wasting time in love. Nothing for which to pat ourselves on the back. And who else will think much of us for just sitting there: Lord, tell her to get up and help.[4] And what do we have. Nothing (but God himself!). We let go of all our doing and thinking and planning, even our thoughts. Our thoughts are the last bastion of the false self. Take away everything else from me, at least I know what I think. But in Centering Prayer we give up even our thoughts. This goes right to the heart of the false self. The prevailing philosophy of our times claims: *Cogito, ergo sum*, I think, therefore I am. This is really just the opposite of

4. Lk 10:40.

reality: I am—a human person by God's wondrous mercy and creation—and therefore I think. Our false self tries to create ourselves with our own thoughts. But in Centering we give up on this project. We let go of the false self; we die to the false self to live to God.

And what freedom we find. We no longer have to worry about what others think. We know how precious we are in the eyes of God. If others do not appreciate us, they are really missing something. We are free. We can do all things in him who strengthens us. We can have all we want, for he has said, 'Ask and you shall receive'. All is ours and we are Christ's and Christ is God's. Alleluia!

No wonder we are filled with joy and peace and truly want to love everyone and care for everyone. Natively speaking, we have a certain listening, a certain way in which we allow life and all that is to speak to us. It is a listening formed by a thousand antecedents. If we are a very prejudiced person, the boundaries of our listening are very fixed. Only what fits within them do we really hear and that is little enough. If we are striving to be more open, then other persons and new experiences can come along and stretch our boundaries and we can hear more, little by little. But there is still so much that cannot fit within. And God—how little of his immense goodness and love we perceive. But when we come to Centering Prayer, we drop all our boundaries. We do not try to fit God or anyone or anything into our ideas or concepts or images. We let all of these go. We sit there, open and vulnerable, and allow the Divine to invade us and stretch us, or better, totally to draw us out into the immensity of his own being.

There is nothing outside now. It is all within. We find everyone within the same Divine Center. We are all one. This is why Centering Prayer so empowers ministry. We come to each and every person as our very self. Love your neighbor *as yourself* (Not, 'as if she were yourself' but as yourself; she is yourself in the oneness we are in Christ). We know we are one in God. My neighbor is myself. How can I not want for her all that I want for myself. It is impossible not to. We are one.

Centering Prayer is a deeply healing prayer. As I rest there deeply in the Lord, the free flow of thoughts and memories— of which I have virtually no awareness, for my attention is wholly set on the Lord even though my rational mind is still functioning—is washing away the hurts and pains, the scars and wounds, the psychological bindings of the past, the past deeply buried in my psyche and now allowed freely to flow up and out. 'Come to me you who are heavily burdened and I will refresh you.' Jesus is still the physician who comes to heal those who have need. In Centering we lay ourselves completely open to his healing ministry, not placing any of our limitations on what he can do. Our psychological defenses are all down. We are wide open. And little by little, as we faithfully center day after day, the healing goes on till we find in our lives a new freedom to love ourselves and everyone else, for now we see ourselves as one with everyone else, the beautiful one reflected in the eyes of the Beloved.

This is the inner reality of the mystery of Church, this is the ultimate meaning of Eucharist. It is really only those who have come to this contemplative insight who can truly understand what it is to pray as Church, what it is to enter into Eucharist.

RECOMMENDATIONS FOR FURTHER READING

A Place Apart: Monastic Prayer and Practice for Everyone. Garden City, N.Y.: Doubleday. 1983.

Centering Prayer: Renewing an Ancient Christian Prayer Form. Garden City, N.Y.: Image. 1982.

Challenges in Prayer. Wilmington, Del.: Michael Glazier. 1982.

Daily We Touch Him: Practical Religious Experiences. Garden City, N.Y.: Doubleday. 1979.

Finding Grace at the Center. Still River, Mass.: St. Bede Publications. 1978.

The Manual of Life: The New Testament for Daily Living. New York: Paulist Press. 1985.

TWO WAYS OF PRAYING

Daily Prayer in Cathedral and Monastery

Paul F. Bradshaw

I N STUDYING the daily public worship of fourth-century Christians, scholars like to draw a distinction between what they call 'cathedral' and 'monastic' types of prayer. This distinction is not primarily based on the *place* in which the worship was offered—'cathedral' worship was not restricted to cathedrals, and 'monastic' worship was not always found in monasteries—but rather on the variations in external *forms* of that worship, and more importantly on the significant differences of the *inner spirit and understanding* of prayer expressed by those divergent forms. Such a distinction, however, has a much wider application. As I intend to show, these two different concepts of the nature of prayer are not just features of the fourth-century Church but can be found throughout christian history and thus have an important part to play in our understanding of prayer today. But first, let us take a look at two examples of 'cathedral' and 'monastic' prayer in their classical, fourth-century, context.

CATHEDRAL PRAYER

We are fortunate in having a quite detailed description of a 'cathedral' style of prayer in part of a travel-diary written by a pilgrim who visited Jerusalem in the last quarter of the fourth century. She appears to have been a nun from western France or Spain named Egeria, who wanted to provide an account of what she saw for the other members of her religious community back home. Although the worship at Jerusalem was not entirely typical of other fourth-century centers of Christianity, and although our visitor may not have been accurate in every detail of her description, even so her account will suffice to convey the general spirit of 'cathedral' prayer.

> Loving sisters, I am sure that it will interest you to know about the daily services they have in the holy places, and I must tell you about them. Every day before cockcrow all the doors of the Anastasis [the Church of the Resurrection] are opened, and the *monazontes* [monks] and *parthenae* [nuns], as they call them here, all enter, and not only these but also lay men and women besides who wish to keep quite an early vigil. From that time until dawn hymns are recited and psalms with their refrains, and antiphons too . . .
>
> When it begins to get light, they begin to recite the morning hymns. Then the bishop comes with his clergy and immediately enters the cave, and from inside the screen he first recites the prayer for all, and he himself commemorates any names he wishes: then he blesses the catechumens. He recites another prayer and blesses the faithful. After this, the bishop comes outside the screen, and all come to his hand, and he blesses them one by one as he comes out, and so the dismissal takes place when it is already light.
>
> Likewise at the sixth hour all again enter the Anastasis, and psalms and antiphons are recited while the bishop is sent for; and again he enters, and does not sit, but immediately goes inside the screen in the Anastasis—that is, the cave where he went earlier—and from there he again first recites a prayer; he then blesses the faithful, and comes outside the screen, and again they come to his hand. The ninth hour is the same as the sixth hour.
>
> At the tenth hour—what they call here *Lychnikon* but we call *Lucernare*—all the people gather again in the Anastasis,

and the lamps and candles are all lit, and the light is very bright. The light is not brought from outside, but is taken from inside the cave, that is, from inside the screen, where a lamp is always burning night and day. The *Lucernare* psalms and antiphons are recited for some time. Then the bishop is sent for, and he enters and takes his seat, and the presbyters also sit in their places. Hymns and antiphons are recited. When they have finished them according to their custom, the bishop rises and stands in front of the screen—that is, the cave—and one of the deacons makes the commemoration of individuals according to the custom, and when the deacon says the names of individuals, a large group of boys always respond, *Kyrie eleison*, or as we say, 'Lord, have mercy'. Their voices are very loud. When the deacon has finished all that he has to say, the bishop first recites a prayer and prays for all. So far the faithful and catechumens pray together. Now the deacon bids all the catechumens to stand where they are and bow their heads, and the bishop then recites the blessing over the catechumens from his place. There is another prayer, and again the deacon bids all the faithful to stand and bow their heads. The bishop then blesses the faithful, and so the dismissal takes place at the Anastasis, and individuals come to his hand. . . .

MONASTIC PRAYER

At about the same time as Egeria was visiting Jerusalem, a monk by the name of John Cassian was observing monastic practices in Egypt, where the monastic movement was born. He later settled in Gaul, and there he wrote a description of egyptian monasticism for the benefit of the local religious communities. Although again the details of his account may not be historically reliable (in particular, he appears to have mingled together the practices of Upper—southern—Egypt with the somewhat different customs of Lower—northern—Egypt), yet he manages to capture the essentials of the ideal spirit of their daily devotions:

Therefore, as we have said, throughout the whole of Egypt and the Thebaid the number of psalms is fixed at twelve in both their evening and the nocturnal celebrations, and two readings follow, one from the Old Testament and one from the New. . . .

These aforesaid prayers, therefore, they begin and end in such a way that, when the psalm is over, they do not immediately hasten to kneel down, as some of us do in this country. . . . Among them, then, it is not so, but before they bend their knees, they pray for a while, and spend the greater part of the time standing for prayer. And so after this, they prostrate themselves on the ground for the shortest space of time, as if adoring the divine mercy, and rise up as quickly as possible, and again standing up with their hands outstretched in the same manner as they had prayed standing before, they prolong their prayers. . . . But when he who is to 'collect' the prayer rises from the ground, they all get up at the same time, so that no one may presume to bend the knee before he bows down, nor to delay when he has risen from the ground, lest it should be imagined that he has not followed the conclusion of the one who 'collected' the prayer but offered his own. . . .

When, therefore, they gather to celebrate the aforesaid rites, which they call *synaxes*, they are all so silent that, although such a large number of brethren is assembled together, one would think that nobody at all was there except the one standing up in the middle to chant the psalm, and especially when the prayer is completed, for then there is no spitting, no clearing of the throat, no noise of coughing, no sleepy yawning with open mouths and gasping, no groans or sighs to distract those around, and no voice is heard except that of the priest concluding the prayer. . . .

Therefore, they do not try to complete the psalms which they sing in the assembly with continuous recitation, but they divide them into two or three sections, according to the number of verses, with prayers in between, and work through them bit by bit. For they do not care about the quantity of verses, but about the intelligence of the mind, adhering strongly to this: 'I will sing with the spirit; I will sing also with the mind'. And so they think it better for ten verses to be sung with thoughtful understanding than for a whole psalm to be poured forth with a bewildered mind. . . .

CONTRASTS

As these two accounts suggest, there are some sharp contrasts between 'cathedral' and 'monastic' types of prayer. I would like to draw attention to five of these.

First of all, 'cathedral' prayer is something that the whole congregation does. They sing the hymns and psalms together as an expression of their corporate praise. Even though an individual cantor might chant the verses themselves, the congregation responds to each one with a refrain. Similarly, the intercessions which follow are an expression of their common concerns. At least at the evening hour in Egeria's description, each petition that is announced by the deacon is greeted with a congregational response, as the people make it their own. Worship is thus essentially communal, or rather ecclesial; for this is not just a prayer-group, it is the Church at prayer. This explains why the presence or absence of an individual from the assembly was a matter of relative indifference in this tradition, and except when it was their turn to perform one of the liturgical functions, even ordained ministers seemingly had no special obligation to be there above that of anyone else. What matters is that the Church should pray, not that every individual should participate in it.

'Monastic' prayer, on the other hand, is fundamentally an individual activity. Although it may appear to be communal from Cassian's account, in reality there was nothing inherently corporate about it, nothing which absolutely required the presence of others, nothing which might not be done equally as well alone as together. Indeed, while the custom in Upper Egypt was for the community to meet together twice every day to pray, as Cassian's description claims, in Lower Egypt the daily prayers were said by the monks individually in their cells.

Thus, although a communal assembly offered an element of mutual encouragement in the work of prayer, and afforded opportunity for supervision and discipline over the possible weakness and indolence of the more junior brethren, gathering together was ultimately a matter of indifference. That is why early monastic rules require each person to be present at every single hour of prayer prescribed in the rule, or if that were not possible, to make up the prayer that was missed on his/her own. It was not enough that the rest of the community had prayed: if the individual did not participate in it, his/her own prayer had not been said.

A second way in which the two traditions of praying differ is in their understandings of liturgical ministry. In 'cathedral' prayer, worship is led by the ordained ministers of the local church: it is presided over by the bishop, or in his absence a presbyter; the intercessions are announced by a deacon; and, although it is not obvious from Egeria's description, the verses of the psalms and canticles are also sung by formally appointed cantors. In 'monastic' prayer, however, there are no permanently designated ministries, but each individual in the community has both the right and the obligation at assemblies for prayer to take an equal turn at chanting the verses of the psalms to the others.

A third contrast between the two ways of praying is in the contents of the prayer. 'Cathedral' prayer is composed chiefly of praise and intercession, the praise being expressed in a limited number of appropriate psalms and canticles, usually unchanging from day to day. Participants saw themselves as engaged the Church's primary priestly vocation, participating in the prayer of Christ, the great high-priest, and continually offering the sacrifice of praise and thanksgiving to God on behalf of all creation and interceding for the salvation of the world. It may rightly be described, therefore, as intrinsically outward-looking in its orientation. It is prayer for others, not just for the benefit of the participants.

The heart of 'monastic' prayer, on the other hand, is essentially silent meditation. The psalms and scripture readings which occur within the rite simply provide the 'food', as it were, for that prayer: the real praying goes on in the spaces in between. The worshipper listens to the words of the psalm or biblical reading, engages in interior reflection on its meaning, and prays for the grace necessary to grow spiritually. 'Monastic' prayer may therefore legitimately be described as pedagogical or formational in its intent. It is inward-looking, directed towards the individual's sanctification. For that reason, it tends to involve a much larger number of psalms than the 'cathedral' tradition, and other scripture readings too, since it tries to draw upon the richness of the biblical treasury to promote this ascetical progress. Indeed, it rapidly became common in early monasticism for a novice to be required to learn the whole Psalter by heart, and for the daily offices to be composed of a cycle of psalms in their biblical order which sought to complete all one hundred and fifty of them within a set period of time.

'Cathedral' and 'monastic' prayer also differ in their 'outward' and 'inward' orientation in another sense. The externals of worship are vitally important to 'cathedral' prayer. Indeed, it is not so much that cathedral prayer is expressed or somehow clothed in the externals, but that the externals are themselves an intrinsic part of the prayer. Note, for example, the attention Egeria pays to the lights at the evening service. It was not just that the Church of the Resurrection was particularly dark and thus required plenty of illumination so that people could see what they were doing. Rather, as we know from other sources, the ritual lighting of the lamps was an important part of evening worship in many parts of the fourth-century Church. As darkness fell, christian communities assembled for prayer, lit the lamps and gave thanks to God for the gift of the natural light of the day which they had enjoyed, for the gift of lamplight to scatter the darkness and terror of the night, and for the gift of the light of the world, Jesus Christ. Often the hymn

'Hail, gladdening light', still used by many Christians today, was sung at this moment. Thus words and actions went together in the 'cathedral' tradition. Similarly, we find that incense too is beginning to be used in worship at about this time, symbolizing the prayers of the saints rising up to heaven (see Ps 141:2; Rev 8:3–4).

For 'monastic' prayer, on the other hand, the externals are ultimately dispensable. The opposite may appear to be the case from Cassian's account, since considerable attention seems to have been directed towards the various postures (standing, kneeling, sitting) to be adopted at different points in the service. But this is misleading. It should be noted that while this common posture is insisted upon, there is no other sign of ceremonial in the service. There is, for example, no ritual lighting of the lamp at the evening office and no use of incense. The changing posture is certainly valued here as an aid to prayer, and the insistence upon concerted action helps to discipline the novice in prayer. But these things are not the prayer itself: 'real' prayer in this tradition is interior, what goes on inside the heart and mind of the worshipper, to which the exterior action may be an aid or support, but one which can eventually be left behind. Once the morning office is over, the same prayer can be continued while sitting plaiting ropes or performing other manual tasks in the Egyptian monastic communities, whereas 'cathedral' prayer cannot.

Finally, one other difference may be mentioned. Both traditions believed firmly in the apostolic injunction, 'pray without ceasing' (1 Thess 5:17). The 'monastic' tradition, however, tends to interpret this literally and thus seeks to spend as much time as possible in actual prayer: the egyptian desert fathers, for example, strove to spend all of their waking hours in prayer, and kept the period of sleep to a minimum, and later monastic orders multiplied the number of offices to be said each day so as to increase the time allocated to prayer. The 'cathedral' tradition of prayer, on the other hand, was content with only occasional assemblies for prayer, usually just twice a day, morning and evening, though sometimes more frequently. Yet this was not to abandon the scriptural precept of ceaseless prayer. For this command was understood to mean not that a Christian should spend as much time as humanly possible in actual praying but that the whole of life should be turned, as it were, into a prayer: 'whether you eat or drink or do any other thing, do all to the glory of God' (1 Cor 10:31).

LATER HISTORY

These two contrasting patterns of prayer were not, as I have already suggested, just something that belonged to fourth-century Christianity. On the contrary, they have both been characteristic of christian prayer throughout its history. Although the particular details of the practices found in the early Church are not always reproduced in later centuries, the different acts of worship tend to resemble one type more than the other. Thus, some were clearly communal actions; in other cases, while a large number of people may have been gathered together in the same physical location, what was going on is really individual worship. For example, while the principal Sunday service of many churches in various christian traditions was generally 'cathedral' in character, in other cases it leaned more in the direction of 'monastic' worship, with the emphasis falling on the reading and preaching of scripture and inner reflection on it by the members of the congregation. And even those christian traditions where the Sunday liturgy was of a 'cathedral' kind often included in their regular weekly cycle other acts of worship which more closely mirrored the 'monastic' pattern, where nothing was done together which could not equally well have been done by each person alone.

Frequently a particular act of worship was composed of elements from both categories. This was the case, for example, in the daily offices celebrated by most religious communities throughout history, which included both reflective psalmody and reading of the 'monastic' kind and also corporate praise and prayer of a 'cathedral' nature. Moreover, sometimes different groups of people would have experienced the same event in different ways. At a medieval high mass, for instance, the clergy and other ministers in the sanctuary no doubt saw themselves as constituting the Church at prayer, engaged in the corporate celebration of its official liturgy; the lay men and women in the congregation, on the other hand, would have experienced the event quite differently, as they got on with their private devotions, pausing only to focus on what was going on in the sanctuary at the solemn moments when bells were rung to attract their attention.

APPLICATION

The same two types can still be discerned in ways of praying today. Thus, some church services resemble more closely the 'cathedral' model, and others the 'monastic'. Some prayer-groups tend in the direction of one pattern, and others the other. Even an individual's prayers may have features of one tradition rather than the other. More often, however, as in the past, forms of worship are a combination of the two ways of praying. And this is not necessarily a bad thing, for both are essential parts of a balanced diet of prayer for Christians. To neglect one or other is to risk a serious deficiency in one's prayer life, even though different human beings may be drawn more naturally to one or the other. Those who find individual contemplation, the saying of the rosary or the stations of the cross, or participation in a charismatic prayer-group most appealing to their spiritual temper also need to take part in the more formal, corporate worship of the Church, offering praise and intercession for others, if they are to share in the fullness of Christianity; conversely, those whose spiritual diet is exclusively composed of liturgical worship also need to find time to explore quiet meditation and reflection if they are to grow into the mind of Christ.

A happy balance, however, is not always what people encounter. The christian tradition in the West, in all traditions, has sadly tended to value one way of prayer more than the other. The meditative road of 'monastic' prayer has been seen as the way for the really 'spiritual' individual, and liturgical worship regarded as much inferior to it. Participation in liturgy, it has been thought, is a christian obligation which of course cannot be neglected, but it is private prayer which is truly beneficial. We can see this trend most clearly in the emergence of the so-called *devotio moderna* in the West at the end of the fourteenth century, which stressed the value of the interior over the exterior in praying and suggested that public worship could present a distraction to 'real' praying. In the centuries that followed, this attitude permeated both Catholic and Protestant traditions in various ways, and can be seen, for example, in the wealth of 'spiritual classics' which emanated in the former and in the growth of Pietism in the latter. Yet until the nineteenth century, it remained largely the preserve of a spiritual elite within Christianity, and it is only since that time that is has spread to become virtually an unquestioned axiom. To accept this situation, however, is to ignore the fact that private prayer tends to be inward-looking, individualistic, and to lack an ecclesial dimension. Valuable though it certainly is in itself, it needs to be supplemented by the experience of liturgical worship for a healthy christian spirituality.

Besides the problem of balance, there is also a second difficulty which often prevents the two ways of prayer from enjoying a peaceful coexistence, and that is a common failure to recognize the difference between them, and therefore to apply the wrong criteria to them. For example, we may attend an act of worship and complain afterwards that there was insufficient opportunity for silent reflection, too much active participation, too much noise from children, and so on. In so doing, we are applying the criteria appropriate to 'monastic' prayer to a service which may have been intended as 'cathedral' worship. Conversely, clergy may be baffled when a large number of their congregation seem to prefer to attend the quiet 8 AM celebration of the eucharist on a Sunday morning instead of the more lively 10 AM service, with more active participation, hymns, and a fellowship hour afterwards. They may even try to introduce some of these things into the early service, thinking that the congregation is missing out on what constitutes real eucharistic worship, and encounter inexplicable opposition to such things as the mutual exchange of a liturgical handshake. They are assuming that what is going on—or should be going on—is 'cathedral' worship, whereas the members of the congregation may well be searching instead for an experience of 'monastic' prayer that newly introduced liturgical changes are denying them.

Like the notion of the four food-groups in dietary planning, therefore, the scholarly distinction between the two types of worship can be an important practical aid in helping us ensure a balanced and healthy spirituality. Both had something vital to contribute to our understanding of prayer and to our christian living. For it is just as unhealthy to become completely absorbed in the cultivation and sanctification of one's own soul to the exclusion of the world around as it is to become so absorbed in the externals of liturgical practice that one loses hold on the inner spirit which feeds and vitalizes that prayer.

RECOMMENDATIONS FOR FURTHER READING

John Wilkinson, *Egeria's Travels*. London: SPCK 1971, 2nd edn, Jerusalem—Warminster: Ariel, 1981. The extracts above are taken from chapter 24.

John Cassian, *Institutes*. Translation in The Nicene and Post-Nicene Fathers of The Church series, volume 11. Rpt. Grand Rapids: Eerdmans. The extracts above are taken from Book Two, chapters 4, 7, 10, and 11.

Paul F. Bradshaw, 'Cathedral vs. Monastery: The Only Alternatives for the Liturgy of the Hours?' in J. Neil Alexander (ed.), *Time and Community: Studies in Liturgical History and Theology*. Washington DC: Pastoral Press. 1990. Pp. 123–136.

Paul F. Bradshaw, 'Whatever happened to daily prayer?', *Worship* 64 (1990) 10–23.

George Guiver, *Company of Voices*. London: SPCK-New York: Pueblo, 1988.

Armand Veilleux, 'Prayer in the Pachomian Koinonia,' in William Skudlarek (ed.), *The Continuing Quest for God*. Collegeville: Liturgical Press, 1982. Pp. 61–66.

PRAYER OF THE HEART:

Sacrament of the Presence of God

John Breck

THE DEEPEST SADNESS and the greatest joy in Christian life are caused by an innate *longing for God*, a passionate quest for intimate and eternal communion with the Persons of the Holy Trinity. Such longing brings sadness, because in this life it goes largely unfulfilled. Rather than lead to frustration, however, it can produce an ineffable joy nourished by the certitude that ultimately nothing can separate us from the love of God in Christ Jesus, that our desire for union with him will ultimately be answered beyond our most fervent hope. This profoundly spiritual longing is often called 'bright sadness' or 'joyful sorrow' (*charmolupe*). In Christian mystical experience, it is the impulse that leads, through ascetic struggle and purification, to *theosis* or 'deification'.

Each of us, without exception, bears within the inner recesses of our being the 'image' of our Creator. Fashioned in that divine image, the holy fathers declare, we are called to grow toward the divine 'likeness' (Gen 1:27f). In the words of Saint Basil the Great, the human person 'is an animal who received the command to become god',[1] that is, to become

---

1. Quoted by Saint Gregory Nazianzus, *Oration* 43. *Cf.* Basil's *Treatise on the Holy Spirit* IX.25: the human vocation is *theon genesthai*.

participants in the very life of God through the deifying power
of the divine 'energies' or operations of the indwelling Spirit.
The motivating force behind this sublime vocation is *eros* or
epithymia, an intense longing or deep affective desire for union
with the Beloved. Perverted by sin, that longing becomes
narcissistic, and the soul goes 'whoring after other gods', idols
fabricated in her own image. Purified by grace, the soul is
redirected toward the original Object of her love. Like the
Prodigal, she turns back home, in repentance and compunction (*penthos*), to discover the Father waiting for her with
open arms. The love that inspires her return, however, is a
response to the prior love of God. 'This is love,' the apostle
tells us, 'not that we loved God, but that he loved us, and sent
his Son as an expiation for our sins' (1 Jn 4:10). Acquisition
of the divine likeness, then, is predicated entirely on divine
initiative. The longing of the soul for eternal life, like that life
itself, is a gift of grace, wholly dependent on the Object of its
affection.

The first prayer of thanksgiving after communion, in the
Liturgy of Saint John Chrysostom, declares: 'Thou art the
true desire and the ineffable joy of those who love, thee, O
Christ our God, and all creation hymns thy praise forever!'
The longing for communion with God is a major incentive
to prayer, which may be described as 'conversation' with
God at the level of the heart. Prayer in the first instance
involves praise and glorification of God, and it includes personal
supplication as well as intercession on behalf of others. Prayer
marked by the intense longing that leads to union with the
Divine, on the other hand, requires *silence*. In addition to
the scriptures, the liturgy, and other sources of revelation
recognized by the Church, Christian mystical tradition has
always known another avenue of divine self-disclosure: God
reveals himself in the silence of the heart. In his letter to the
Magnesians, Saint Ignatius of Antioch declared, 'There is one
God who manifested himself through Jesus Christ his Son,

who is his Word, proceeding from silence.'[2] Saint Isaac the Syrian expressed a similar thought with his familiar statement, 'Silence is the sacrament of the world to come; words are the instrument of this present age.'[3] Revelation that communicates knowledge of God requires words, as do petitions that address needs and conditions of our daily life. Prayer uttered out of the deepest longing for God, however, demands silence.

Yet silence, at least in present times, seems to be the most difficult of virtues to acquire. We fear it, and we run from it in a relentless search for noise and distraction. A stroll on the beach requires the companionship of a 'walkman'. At the workplace, or waiting on the phone, or shopping for groceries, we expect to be 'entertained' by music—any music, so long as it focuses our attention outside ourselves and away from our inner being. Silence means a void, a dreadful emptiness that demands to be filled. What we choose to fill that void with most often produces, not only noise, but agitation through over-stimulation. Sensory overload is addictive. It becomes an escape from the present, from the self, from God. Like any addiction, it is pathological and life-threatening. From the news media to MTV to contemporary works of art, American culture is marked by an insatiable hunger for stimuli that divert our attention from 'the place of the heart', the place of inner silence and solitude. To some degree, however, this has always been the case. When Adam was cast forth from the Garden, he lost more than life in paradise. He lost the gift of silence, and with it he lost 'the language of the world to come'.

In human experience prayer offers the way to recover that language, for authentic prayer transcends human language and issues in the silence of God. It is this intuition, confirmed by

---

2. *Letter to the Magnesians* VII.2.

3. Letter 3. Recall the ancient hymn, sung in the byzantine tradition at the Great Entrance of the Holy Saturday Liturgy: 'Let all mortal flesh keep silence . . . .'

ecclesial experience, that led ancient spiritual guides to develop what is called 'hesychast' prayer. The term *hesychia* signifies inner calm, stillness, silence. It describes not so much a method as an attitude, a disposition of mind and heart which facilitates remembrance of God and concentration upon him to whom prayer is directed.

In its earliest expression, hesychast prayer took the form of ejaculatory petitions, single words or phrases fired like an arrow towards God. *Marana tha!*, 'Our Lord, Come!' may be one of the earliest examples, together with Peter's cry as he sank in the waters of the lake of Galilee, 'Lord, save me!'[4] These and similar petitions could be spoken aloud in the church assembly or repeated silently by someone praying in solitude. From virtually the time of the resurrection, however, special emphasis was placed on the name of Jesus, as having unique, life-giving power. 'There is salvation in no one else [but Jesus Christ], for there is no other Name under heaven given among men by which we must be saved.'[5] The name 'Jesus', given by the angel at the Annunciation, signifies 'God is salvation'. It was, therefore, very naturally taken up and incorporated into such brief, frequently repeated petitions.

Gradually, out of the experience of the desert monastics during the fourth and fifth centuries, there grew a more or less fixed formula that we know as 'the Jesus Prayer': *Lord Jesus Christ, Son of God, have mercy on me, a sinner.*[6] In this

---

4. 1 Cor 16:23, Rev 22:20; Mt 14:30.

5. Acts 4:12. See the monograph by Bishop Kallistos Ware, *The Power of the Name* (Fairacres, Oxford: SLG Press, 1974).

6. *Kyrie Iesou Christe huie tou theou, eleeson me [ton hamartolon].* Kallistos Ware, 'The Jesus Prayer in St Gregory of Sinai,' *Eastern Churches Review* IV/1 (1972) 12 and note 44, locates the origin of the 'standard' formula in the 'Life of Abba Philemon' from sixth-seventh-century Egypt, but without the final phrase, 'a sinner'. It existed in many other forms, the most primitive of which, as he notes, may have been simply invocation of the name: 'Lord Jesus'.

classic form, it combines a doctrinal confession ('Jesus is Lord') with a supplication that seeks forgiveness and healing.[7] Because some persons receive the grace by which this simple formula is gradually internalized, becoming rooted in the innermost sanctuary of one's being, it is virtually synonymous with 'prayer of the heart'.

The Jesus Prayer is often said to have originated in the context of the hesychast movement associated with Saint Gregory Palamas and Athonite monks of the thirteenth and fourteenth centuries. 'Palamism', however, must be seen as the culmination of a long tradition which begins with the Holy Scriptures. In one form or another the Prayer was practiced by anchorites of Syria, Palestine, and Egypt during the fourth and fifth centuries. It flourished on Mount Sinai under the spiritual direction of Saint John of the Ladder from the sixth century, then on Mount Athos from the tenth century. Only some four hundred years later did the Prayer become the focus of the controversy between Gregory Palamas (d. 1359) and Barlaam the Calabrian. By the fifteenth century the Jesus Prayer had become the cornerstone of much Russian Orthodox piety, finally inspiring the nineteenth-century classic known as *The Way of a Pilgrim*.[8] During the second half of the preceding

7. The Greek term for 'mercy' (*eleeson*) is closely related to the word for 'oil' (*elaion*). The petition 'have mercy on me', like the *Kyrie eleison* that serves as a leitmotif of the Eastern liturgies, is in effect a request that God anoint the individual or community with 'the oil of gladness'. It recalls the wine and oil applied by the Good Samaritan in Jesus' parable (Lk 10:34), with its properties of purification and healing.

8. The best-known english translation of this work is by R. M. French (London, 1954). Numerous other editions have appeared in recent years. The first four chapters consist of a spiritual biography of a handicapped russian peasant who undertakes a spiritual pilgrimage toward (the heavenly) Jerusalem. It recounts his experience with the Jesus Prayer, which he learns to interiorize through constant repetition guided by a spiritual father. The last three chapters ('The Pilgrim Continues His Way') offer an in-depth meditation on the nature of hesychast prayer.

century, Nicodemus of the Holy Mountain ('the Hagiorite'), together with his friend Macarius of Corinth, enshrined traditional teaching on the Jesus Prayer in five tomes entitled the *Philokalia* (first translated into Russian by Paisy Velichkovsky as *Dobrotolubiye*).[9] The complete collection contains sayings from the fathers on prayer, beginning with Anthony the Great (d. 356) and concluding with Gregory Palamas, thus embracing more than a millennium of eastern contemplative tradition. The title of the work *Philokalia*, signifies 'love of beauty'. The expression conveys the truth about the divine life and purpose which the heart learns through practice of the Prayer. God is love; he is also the source of all that is truly beautiful, resplendent with divine glory. Such beauty, the Russian philosophers held, 'will save the world'.

THE BIBLICAL FOUNDATION OF THE JESUS PRAYER

In answer to the Pharisee's question as to when the Kingdom would come, Jesus replied, 'The Kingdom of God is not coming with observable signs . . . behold, the Kingdom of God is within you' (Lk 17:20–21). While most modern commentators take the greek expression *entos hymon* to mean 'among you', 'in your midst'—that is, as present in Jesus' person—patristic interpreters tended to render it 'within you'. From this point of view, the Kingdom is a mystical reality, a divine gift to be cherished and cultivated within the inward being, in the depths of the secret heart. Access to that inner reality is provided by prayer, particularly continual prayer that centers upon the divine Name.

Such prayer, however, must never be treated as a technique, a christianized mantra, whose use enables one to attain a particular spiritual end. Prayer, as Saint Paul insists, can never be

---

9. For a useful overview of the respective contributions of Macarius and Nicodemus, see K. Ware, 'The Spirituality of the Philokalia,' in *Sobornost* 13/1 (1991) 6–24.

manipulated, since in its essence it is not a human undertaking at all. 'We do not know how to pray as we should,' he declares, 'but the Spirit himself intercedes for us with groanings too deep for words' (Rom 8:26). True prayer occurs when the Spirit addresses the Father, 'Abba,' in the temple of the human heart. It is essentially a divine activity. Yet like every aspect of the spiritual life, it demands *synergeia* or co-operation on our part. To attain *theoria*, the contemplative vision of God, one must proceed by way of *praxis*, active struggle toward purification and acquisition of virtue through obedience to the divine commandments.

Prayer, then, is not merely a gift; it is work. It demands patience, persistence and ascetic discipline. It also demands the constant vigilance known as *nepsis* or 'watchfulness'. The hebrew sage admonished, 'Watch over your heart with all diligence, for from it flow the springs of life'.[10] 'Watch!,' Jesus commanded his disciples at the close of his apocalyptic warnings. 'What I say to you, I say to all: Watch!' (Mk 13:33–37). Such watchfulness raises a bulwark against demonic images (*phantasiai*) or thoughts (*logismoi*), enabling the mind and heart to concentrate on 'the one thing needful' (cf. Lk 10:42). More than by any other virtue, we co-operate with God in the activity of prayer through *nepsis*. This is the attitude of sober vigilance exemplified by the five virgins who welcomed the Bridegroom, and by the maiden who awaited her lover: 'I slept, but my heart kept watch'.[11]

Prayer, then, requires our co-operation with the Spirit of God through 'a watchful mind, pure thoughts, and a sober heart'.[12] With this conviction, the fathers turned to Holy Scripture in order to discern various levels of prayer that can

10. Prov 4:23, New American Standard translation.
11. Mt 25:1–13; Song of Songs 5:2.
12. From the 'Evening Prayer to Christ' of the byzantine Compline service.

be attained in the spiritual life. A key passage is I Timothy 2:1, 'First of all, I urge that petitions, prayers, intercessions, and thanksgivings be made on behalf of all.' To the patristic mind these represented four stages, or orders, of prayer, from the most elementary to the most sublime.[13] The apostle first names 'petitions' or 'supplications' (deëseis). These include confession of sins, together with requests for spiritual cleansing and wholeness. Their thrust is basically therapeutic, seeking liberation from all that impedes progress toward perfection. Second, he speaks of 'prayers' (proseuchas), meaning positive requests for the gifts and fruit of the Spirit, for virtue and the attainment of righteousness. The third order or level consists of 'intercessions' (enteuxeis). At this stage, one turns from one's own spiritual concerns to focus on the needs of others through intercession; this is in essence a prayer of mediation that seeks another's salvation. Finally, one reaches the level of 'thanksgivings' (eucharistias), in which the heart rises toward God in joyous adoration, offered in response to his saving grace.

Yet, as the fathers insist, the four stages exist simultaneously in the spiritual life. Thanksgiving must be complemented by ongoing repentance and petition for the forgiveness of sin, just as intercessions on behalf of others go hand in hand with prayers for one's self. Beyond these four levels or orders of prayer, however, there is another about which we can say virtually nothing; yet we shall have to return to it when we raise the question of the way hesychast prayer is internalized. This ultimate form or degree is known as kathara proseuche, 'pure prayer', which issues from the ineffable experience of

13. Examples of this kind of exegesis can be found in many sources. On the question in general, see especially The Art of Prayer, ed. Igumen Chariton of Valamo (London: Faber, 1966), with an excellent introduction by Kallistos Ware; and Unseen Warfare by Lorenzo Scupoli, ed. by Nicodemus of the Holy Mountain, revised by Theophan the Recluse (Crestwood, NY: St Vladimir's Seminary Press, 1978).

union with God, in peace, love and joy. Although it defies any attempt to express it with words or images (all of which inevitably deteriorate into *logismoi* and *phantasiai*), it is the truest prayer of all, the utterance of the Spirit himself. As unitive prayer, it is both the goal and the fulfillment of *hesychia*.

A key element in hesychasm is frequent repetition: continual prayer as a means to uninterrupted and ever deeper communion with God. The psalmist declared, 'I keep the Lord always before me; because he is at my right hand, I shall not be moved' (Ps 15/16:8). The apostle Paul exhorts his followers to 'pray without ceasing' (*adialeiptos proseuchesthe*, 1 Thess 5:17), urging them to persevere, seeking constancy in prayer (*tei proseuchei proskarterountes*, Rom 12:12).[14]

Both the object and the content of such repetitive prayer is the divine *Name*. According to hebrew thought, a name expresses the essence of the person or thing that bears it. By extension, knowing the name of an adversary gives some measure of control over him. The patriarch Jacob wins the struggle with the angel of God, then immediately seeks to learn his name. Although the angel refuses to divulge it, he bestows upon Jacob the new name 'Israel', prophetically announcing the salvation of God's elect people (Gen 32:27–29). Jesus gains power over demons by asking their name: 'Legion is my name,' he/they reply, 'for we are many' (Mk 5:1–20). In this same encounter, the demons identify Jesus by name, adding a christological confession which even his disciples were not capable of making: 'What is your concern with me, Jesus, Son of the Most High God?' Our name reveals our authentic identity, the innermost reality or truth (*aletheia*) of our being. Accordingly, Moses seeks to learn the name of God at the theophany on Mount Sinai. As he will with Jacob, God refuses

---

14. The same idea is expressed in Col 4:2, 'Be constant in prayer'; and he adds, 'being watchful (*gregorountes*) in it with thanksgiving.'

to give his Name. Instead, he affirms the truth of his being: 'I AM' (*ego eimi*, Exod 3:13–15).[15] In philosophical language, this is an existential rather than an ontological identification. Nothing is revealed of the divine essence, the inner being of the Godhead. Rather, God declares that he IS: Yahweh is the God who is present and active within human life and experience.

Yet the Name he does reveal to Moses conveys all the truth about God that can ever be known or expressed. 'I AM,'' he declares. 'This is my Name forever.' In the person of the incarnate Son, God continues to manifest himself as 'I AM'. The revelatory formula 'Be not afraid!' is often coupled with the added word, 'I AM'. Translations that render *ego eimi* as 'It is I' do a great disservice. They obscure the point that in encounters with Jesus—whether they occur to the disciples on the Sea of Galilee (Mt 14:27) or in the upper room on the night of his betrayal (Jn 14:6) or during a resurrection appearance (Lk 24:39, *ego eimi autos*)—the designation 'I AM' signals a theophany, a manifestation of divine life and purpose. God's being is revealed by his acts, and beyond those 'mighty acts' nothing can be known of him. 'I AM the Alpha and the Omega, says the Lord God, who is and was and is to come, the Almighty!' (Rev 1:8).

Prayer of the heart focuses upon the divine Name because that Name itself is a personal theophany, a manifestation of God in Trinity. By invoking the name of Jesus with faith and love, the worshiper ascends Mount Sinai to stand before the divine Presence. Byzantine theologians developed this image of ascent, the passage of the soul through divine darkness to the uncreated light, on the basis of the primal experience

15. The designation I AM is the equivalent of '*ho on*,' '*He* who exists'. This is another form of the divine Name, invoked in the final blessing of the Byzantine office ('Christ our God, the Existing One, is blessed . . .'), and inscribed on icons of the Holy Face.

of God as *personal*. Within the 'immanent Trinity', the inner life of the Godhead, the three Persons exist in an eternal communion of love, united in a common nature and a common will. Accordingly, the Trinity *ad extra*—the 'economic' Trinity which is present and active within creation—reveals itself as three personal realities who bear the 'names' of Father, Son, and Spirit.

Since the name bears and manifests the reality of the one who possesses it, prayer must address God precisely by these revealed names. Orthodox Christianity, therefore, is obliged to retain the traditional language of God's self-disclosure, and to refrain from substituting functional designations such as 'Creator', 'Redeemer', and 'Sanctifier'. 'Inclusive language', while appropriate to eliminate a masculine bias that has affected many of our translations, cannot properly apply to the God-head. This is not only because God is 'beyond gender'. It is primarily because functional 'names' such as these, so prevalent in church usage today, lead inevitably to confusion and distortion, that is, to 'heresy'. However unpopular the label 'heresy' might be, it remains a useful term insofar as it implies a serious distortion of the most basic elements of revelation. Eastern tradition opposes 'inclusive' or 'functional' designations for God for the fundamental reason that the three divine Persons share a common will and activity. The Father is Creator; yet he is the author of redemption and sanctification. The Son is Redeemer; yet he is the agent of creation and the mediator of sanctifying grace. The Spirit is Sanctifier; yet he is the *spiritus creator*, who actualizes within ecclesial experience the redemptive work of the Son. As Saint Gregory Nazianzus declared, the persons of the Godhead can only be distinguished in terms of their *origin*: the Father is eternally 'ungenerated', the Son is eternally 'generated', and the Spirit eternally 'proceeds' from the Father through the Son. Prayer, then, cannot properly address

God with 'functional' language, since such language inevitably obscures the revealed identity of each divine Person.[16]

The name addressed by prayer of the heart is thus a *personal* name, one that reveals both the identity and the purpose of the One who bears it. Most frequently this is a name of the Son of God, the 'Second Person' of the Holy Trinity. The child born of the Virgin receives the name 'Jesus', 'God is salvation'; yet he is also designated 'Emmanuel', meaning 'God is with us' (Mt 1:23, Is 7;14). As the risen and exalted One, he receives the Name above every name: *'Kyrios'* or 'Lord', the Name of God himself (Phil 2:10–11). To Saint Paul, even the title *Christos* or Christ, which originally signified 'the Anointed One' or 'Messiah', had the force of a proper name: 'I have been crucified with Christ; it is no longer I who live, but Christ who lives in me' (Gal 2:19–20). In each case, the name conveys not only the personal identity of the incarnate Son; it also designates his divine 'operation' as saviour, revealer, ruler, or

---

16. Masculine 'names' have traditionally been attributed to the first two divine Persons, and, by association, to the Spirit as well. This usage is preserved today by Orthodox and many other Christians, and is defended on grounds of revelation: in the Old Testament (rarely), but especially in Jesus' own teaching, God is made known as *Abba*, Father; the Logos becomes incarnate as a male; and the Son and the Spirit come forth from the Father, who is identified as the 'source' (*pege*) or 'principle' (*arche*) of all life, both created and uncreated. In antiquity, with very little knowledge of reproductive biology and a patriarchalist environment, the acts of 'generation' and 'bringing forth' ('causing to proceed') were understood as uniquely male functions. Today there is growing appreciation for the *maternal* aspects of God's relation to the world and human persons—and Orthodox theologians themselves are actively exploring the implications of feminine images used of the Spirit in early Syriac Christianity. If orthodox Christians of all stripes insist on retaining masculine names for God, it is because Scripture itself employs such gender-specific designations. God is indeed 'beyond gender'; and all such gender-related names must be seen as analogies. But the limits of human language are not expanded by shifting analogies away from the biblical images, to speak both of and to God as 'Mother'. This carries pagan overtones that seriously distort God's self-disclosure as it is given in the biblical witness.

liberator. To invoke the Name is to invoke as well the saving power inherent in that Name.

Bishop Ignatius Brianchaninov, a widely respected spiritual leader of nineteenth-century Russia, held that the Prayer of Jesus, focusing on the Name, is a 'divine institution' established by the Son of God Himself.[17] He grounds this assertion in Jesus' extraordinary promise made to his disciples in the upper room on the night of his Passion (Jn 14:13f): 'Whatever you ask in my name, I will do it, that the Father may be glorified in the Son; if you ask anything in my name, I will do it'. Later on Jesus adds: 'If you ask anything of the Father in my name, he will give it to you. Hitherto you have asked nothing in my name; ask and you will receive, that your joy may be full' (16:23f). In a similar vein, the author of Hebrews exhorts his listeners: 'Through [Jesus] let us continually offer up a sacrifice of praise to God, that is, the fruit of lips that confess his name' (Heb 13:15). Confession of the name of Jesus is here identified as a 'sacrifice of praise', offered by human lips in gratitude for the life-giving sacrifice offered by our great High Priest on the altar of the cross. A generation later such power had been attributed to the name of Jesus that the unknown author of the *Shepherd of Hermas* could declare, 'The Name of the Son of God is great and without limit; it upholds the whole universe.'[18]

The New Testament also records the ancient linkage made between the divine Name and the appeal for 'mercy'. Saint Luke recounts Jesus' parable in which the tax collector casts his eyes to the ground and beats his breast, imploring, 'O God, have mercy on me, a sinner!' (Lk 18:13). The blind man identified by Saint Mark as 'Bartimaeus' ('son of Timaeus') defies the attempts of the crowd to silence him and cries out,

---

17. See the opening chapter of his remarkable little book, *On the Prayer of Jesus* (London: Watkins, 1952) pp. 2–3: 'Praying by the prayer of Jesus is a divine institution . . . instituted by the Son of God and God Himself'.

18. *Similitudes* 9.14.

'Jesus, Son of David, have mercy on me!' (Mk 10:47). From here it was only a short step to formulate the familiar petition, 'Jesus, Son of God, have mercy on me, a sinner!' Thus the New Testament itself can be considered the primary source of both corporate liturgical worship and individual devotion. The *Kyrie eleison* of the communal liturgy has as its counterpart personal invocation of the Name of Jesus coupled with the petition, 'have mercy on me!'

THE HESYCHAST WAY OF PRAYER

Hesychasm (*hesychia*) may be described as a tradition of prayer, based on inner discipline (*askesis*), that leads to contemplation of the divine presence. Although certain streams of that tradition are associated with a vision of the Uncreated Light, its true aim is to establish communion, in the depths of the heart, with the Persons of the Holy Trinity.

Hesychasm seeks ultimately to attain *theosis* or 'deification', through participation in the 'energies' or operations of God. These consist of divine attributes, such as love, wisdom, justice, beauty. Attainment of this sublime end involves us in an 'antinomy', the apparent paradox of *synergeia* or co-operation with God. On the one hand, human effort is necessary, to respond to divine grace with faith and ascetic effort. This engages us in 'unseen warfare' with sin and temptation, principalities and powers. On the other hand, grace remains a free gift, totally independent of any merit or accomplishment on our part. 'Synergy' consists of divine initiative and human response. The human element, however, is limited to repentance, a constant turning back to God with a broken and contrite heart.[19]

---

19. Hesychast tradition understands repentance to involve 'guarding the heart': "Be attentive to yourself, so that nothing destructive can separate you from the love of God. Guard your heart, and do not grow listless and say: 'How shall I guard it, since I am a sinner?' For when a man abandons his sins and returns to God, his

The apostle Paul declared the body to be a 'temple of the Holy Spirit within you' (1 Cor 6:19). Hesychast tradition knows that temple to be 'the place of the heart'. According to biblical thought, the heart is the center of all life, somatic, psychic, and spiritual. It is the organ of reason, of intelligence, and therefore of knowledge of God. As such it is the most intimate point of encounter between God and the human person.

Hesychast prayer is grounded in a theology of the heart. The recently canonized bishop Theophan Govorov (1815–1894), known as 'the Recluse', expressed the essence of the hesychast way in the following simple yet profound assertions:

> The heart is the innermost person. Here are located self-awareness, the conscience, the idea of God and of one's complete dependence on Him; and all the eternal treasures of the spiritual life.
>
> [True prayer] is to stand *with the mind in the heart* before God, and to go on standing before Him ceaselessly, day and night, until the end of life.[20]

Here there is neither enthusiasm nor quietism,[21] but total sobriety, with a complete integration of the spiritual faculties. Yet once again, although attainment of this state of integration demands an ongoing struggle against the 'passions', the inclinations of the fallen self, it remains wholly dependent on the work of the Holy Spirit. The quality and intensity of prayer that leads to abiding communion with God are bestowed only by the Spirit. Prayer of the heart is a *charismatic* prayer in the

---

repentance regenerates him and renews him entirely." Saint Isaiah the Solitary (5th century), 'On Guarding the Intellect' [text 22], *The Philokalia* vol. 1 (ed. G. E. H. Palmer, Philip Sherrard, Kallistos Ware), (London & Boston: Faber, 1979) p. 26.

20. Theophan the Recluse, *The Art of Prayer*, pp. 190 and 63.

21. On the difference between 'quietism' and the 'quiet' or 'calm' of *hesychia*, see K. Ware, 'Silence in Prayer: The Meaning of Hesychia,' *Theology and Prayer*, ed. A. M. Allchin, Studies Supplementary to *Sobornost*, no. 3 (London: Fellowship of Saint Alban and Saint Sergius, 1975) 21f.

genuine sense of the term. 'We do not know how to pray as we ought . . .' But the Spirit, as a free gift, makes prayer possible. 'The love of God has been poured out into our hearts through the Holy Spirit given to us,' Paul affirms (Rom 5:5). And the chief work of the Spirit is to quicken authentic prayer within us. In the words of the great seventh century Syrian mystic, Isaac of Nineveh:

> When the Spirit takes up His [in Syriac, Her] dwelling place in a man, he never ceases to pray, for the Spirit will constantly pray in him. Then neither when he sleeps nor when he is awake will prayer be cut off from his soul; but when he eats and when he drinks, when he lies down or when he does any work, even when he is immersed in sleep, the perfumes of prayer will breathe in his heart spontaneously.[22]

How does one acquire such prayer? The answer, once again, lies more in the dynamic of 'longing', in a spiritual attitude of love for God and the intense desire to commune with him, than it does in the acquisition of 'techniques'. There are, however, certain steps one can take to create the outer and inner conditions that facilitate genuine prayer, including prayer of the heart. These include achieving a certain measure of silence and solitude, to hear the voice of God and become aware of his presence.

The *Apophthegmata patrum* or *Sayings of the Desert Fathers*, include a familiar story of Saint Arsenius (354–450) that stresses the importance of silence and solitude for acquiring inner prayer. Arsenius sought from God the way to salvation, and a voice replied, 'Flee men! Flee, keep silent, and be still, for these are the roots of sinlessness.'[23] This does not, however,

---

22. *Mystic Treatises by Isaac of Nineveh*, tr. A. J. Wensinck (Amsterdam, 1923; 2nd ed. Wiesbaden, 1967) p. 174.

23. Arsenius, 1.2; PG 65:88BC. *Cf.* Saint John Climacus, *The Ladder of Divine Ascent* 27 (PG 88:1100A), quoted by K. Ware, 'Silence in Prayer,' p. 13: 'Close the door of your cell physically, the door of your tongue to speech, and the inward door to the evil spirits.'

imply rejection of others or isolation for its own sake. Nor does it mean that one no longer listens to others or seeks communion with them. Silence and solitude are inner qualities that imbue all speech and all personal relationships with peace and attentive love. They serve to cultivate a level of spiritual transparency that enables the voice of God to be heard and his presence to be felt, whatever the ambient conditions might be.

With regard to the Jesus Prayer itself, however, two points need to be stressed above all. First, we cannot force the prayer. As a gift of the Holy Spirit, it cannot be manipulated. Any attempt to use the Prayer as a mantra, or to exploit it as a psychological tool for relaxation or for any other proximate goal, will inevitably lead to spiritual shipwreck. And second, if one is to progress along 'the way of hesychast prayer', it is imperative that one be continually guided by a spiritual master. Today we are faced with a dearth of *startsi*, spiritual elders, who can guide the seeker by virtue of their own experience with prayer and ascetic discipline. To a limited extent, books can serve as a substitute: hence the publication and translation of the *Philokalia, The Art of Prayer, The Way of a Pilgrim*, and many other important works that convey the distilled wisdom of centuries of experience. Books, however, need to be used with discretion. Even if their content is *nihil obstat* in the eyes of God, it is always possible for the reader, because of sin, weakness or ignorance, to misconstrue and misuse their wisdom. Any serious quest for attainment of prayer of the heart needs to be guided by someone qualified to do so.

This said, however, it is possible—and highly desirable—for any Christian to make sober and genuinely pious use of the Jesus Prayer. Without attempting to 'produce' prayer of the heart, one can nevertheless incorporate the usual formula, or a shorter version of it, into personal prayer at any time and under any circumstances. Even called upon occasionally, the Name of Jesus manifests its grace and healing power.

When they speak of the actual internalization of the Jesus Prayer, the spiritual masters usually distinguish three stages: oral or verbal, mental, and prayer of the heart. The novice (like the Russian Pilgrim) begins with frequent, unhurried repetition of the prayer, adopting a regular rhythm which may or may not be associated with breathing.[24] One may, for example, form the words 'Lord Jesus Christ, Son of God,' while inhaling, then exhale with 'have mercy on me, a sinner'. Posture can also be an important factor in acquiring a fruitful rhythm and intensity of prayer. Often it is recommended that one sit on a low stool and fix both the gaze and the mental attention literally on the place of the heart, the center or left side of the chest. Pain can often occur as a result of the cramped position. This can have a positive effect insofar as it concentrates attention. If it becomes a hindrance or burden, or is ever sought for its own sake, then it should be avoided as a temptation or even deception (plane). As with all things, discernment is crucial.

The Russian Pilgrim was instructed to pray the Jesus Prayer frequently, finally several thousands of times each day. This is more than most people can manage; it can even be dangerous if it expresses an unconscious compulsion, a need born of 'religiosity' rather than sobriety and a genuine desire to commune with God. Here the crucial element is moderation.

Often one finds that use of a chotki or prayer cord helps considerably in focusing attention and establishing a rhythm of repetition.[25] While it can be used carelessly, like conversation

24. Far too much has been made of the role of the breath in hesychast prayer. While coordinating the prayer with the breath can be useful for some, for others it is a distraction and an obstacle. This, too, needs to be decided with the guidance of an experienced teacher. Saint Theophan the Recluse notes: 'The descent of the mind into the heart by the way of breathing is suggested for the case of anyone who does not know where to hold his attention, or where the heart is; but if you know, without this method, how to find the heart, choose your own way there. Only one thing matters—to establish yourself in the heart.' The Art of Prayer, p. 198.

25. The Orthodox prayer cord is usually made of black wool thread tied in a chain of complicated knots and ending with a cross. It often contains one hundred knots, but that is variable. One seldom uses it to count the number of prayers said.

beads, it should be integrated into the practice of prayer consciously and with respect. Like prostrations and the sign of the cross, it permits involvement of the physical body in the activity of worship.

Gradually as the Prayer is repeated, it begins to transcend the verbal level and root itself in the mind. One continues to pray with the lips. But the Prayer seems to take on a life of its own, whether one is awake or asleep. Many experiences have been told, such as that of a Roman Catholic contemplative sister who slowly regained consciousness after a serious car accident. Before she actually came to, those around her saw her lips forming the words of the Jesus Prayer. 'I slept, but my heart kept watch . . .'.

Once the Prayer is imprinted on the mind, it appears to 'pray itself' spontaneously. The writers of commercial jingles understand all too well the psychological mechanism of memory involved here. With the Prayer, of course, there is a far deeper dimension, one that embraces the entire being, suffusing mind, heart and body with a sense of peace and joy. This is the bright sadness that radiates from the faces of saints depicted in authentic iconography. It is not merely the psyche's response to repetition. It is a gift of the Holy Spirit which calls forth compunction and penitence, love of and devotion for God, and at times, the cleansing, healing grace of tears.

The authors of the *Philokalia*, and countless others with them, know of a still deeper level of prayer called *kathara proseuche* or 'pure prayer'. This ultimate stage is reached when the Prayer literally 'descends from the mind into the heart'. There, as the voice of the Spirit himself, it makes its dwelling place within the inner sanctuary. Then the Prayer is no longer 'prayed' as a conscious, deliberate act. It is received, welcomed,

---

Rather, it serves to focus the mind through a bodily gesture and adds the faculty of touch to the experience of prayer.

and embraced as a manifestation of divine Presence and Life. The Prayer now associates itself with the rhythm of the heart, producing without conscious effort a ceaseless outpouring of adoration and thanksgiving. From prayer of the lips to prayer of the mind, it has become 'prayer of the heart'.

But once again, such prayer is a gift and must always be respected as such. Many have actively sought it, through heroic *praxis*, in the hope of being blessed with the divine vision and knowledge known as *theoria*. Some have been granted the gift almost at once. After only three weeks, Saint Silouan of Athos was so blessed. Saint Symeon the New Theologian (d. 1022) struggled and implored God for years before he received the gift of pure prayer. And many saints, of course, never do. That determination, like salvation itself, must be left entirely in the hands of God. Nevertheless, there is virtue in seeking the gift, whether or not it is accorded, as long as it is sought out of love for God and longing for union with him, and not for the sake of the experience itself. In this regard, discernment of one's motives can also be made most surely and most effectively through the guidance of a spiritual teacher.

THE FRUIT OF THE JESUS PRAYER

The depth and authenticity of prayer are known by its fruits. We can gauge the truth of our own prayer by the effects it has on our personal life and relationships. With respect to the Jesus Prayer, we can conclude by noting four such effects.

In the first place, practice of the Prayer promotes what is referred to today as *centering*. Within the spiritual life, this means focusing on 'the one thing needful' (Lk 10:42). Yet this ability to 'center' is itself a gift, one granted in a relationship of 'synergy' between God and the human person. Mary of Bethany welcomes Jesus into her home and places herself at his feet in the position of a disciple. While her sister Martha busies herself with domestic affairs, Mary seeks what is essential. She centers upon the Word of God, and receives an invaluable legacy, 'the good portion that will not be taken away'. The Prayer of Jesus can serve to focus thought during periods of meditation. Once it becomes an integral part of worship, regardless of its degree of internalization, it produces an ability to concentrate, to center, that provides depth and richness to all prayer.

A second purpose of the Prayer, and fruit born by it, is acquisition of the *memory of God*. Great mystics of the Christian East from Diadochus of Photice in the fifth century to Gregory of Sinai in the fourteenth used the expression 'Memory of God' as equivalent to invocation of the Name of Jesus or 'Prayer of the Heart'.[26] The concept of 'memory', in hebrew thought as well as greek, signifies more than recollection, the recalling of a person or an event. *Anamnesis*, as its use in the Liturgy suggests, signifies 'reactualization'. Through the anamnetic quality of the Liturgy, the saving events of Christ's death and resurrection are rendered present and 'actual' in the experience of the worshiping Church. Repetition of the Prayer of Jesus can have this same anamnetic effect. By it, one 'remembers' God in the sense of rendering him present; or rather, one opens the mind and heart to his presence, otherwise obscured by thoughts, images, and other distractions. To preserve the memory of God is to hold oneself continually in God's presence, with fear and trembling, but also with the certitude that Jesus remains with us 'until the end of the age'.

Practice of the Prayer of Jesus can also bear fruit of *self-sacrificing love*. We are becoming aware today that much self-sacrifice within the Church is the result of religious addiction, a compulsive need to help, heal, and save others, however appropriate or inappropriate our actions might be. Self-sacrifice can in reality be the unconscious sacrifice of one's

26. See K. Ware, 'The Jesus Prayer in St Gregory of Sinai,' p. 17.

family, of friends, and of one's well-being, all in the name of 'fixing' or 'rescuing'. These are destructive behaviors; and often our own discernment is not adequate to distinguish them from genuine expressions of *diakonia*. Yet the fact of such compulsive behaviors should never be allowed to obscure Christ's call to take up one's cross, to go the extra mile, to sacrifice one's own interests out of love and concern for another.

In ways that are not explainable but are a constant in Christian experience, invocation of the Name of Jesus can bring order, harmony and clarity of vision out of our inner chaos. It can restructure our unconscious priorities, so that love is no longer self-serving but is freely offered from a 'pure heart and a sober mind'. Perhaps the Prayer decreases our level of anxiety by causing both mind and heart to surrender to him who is the Wisdom, Word, and Power of God. More accurately, the love that issues from practice of the Prayer is a fruit of the Spirit, together with 'joy, peace . . . and self-control' (Gal 5:22). Both a 'gift' and a 'fruit', that love itself is the power of God, for reconciliation, growth, and healing in every personal relationship.

The fourth effect or fruit of the Prayer of Jesus leads us back to where we began, to the concept of *longing*. Longing for God, the intense inner desire of the heart that seeks eternal union with him, is the driving force and the sanctifying grace of the spiritual life. It provides the courage and strength to assume the ascetic way toward *theosis*, the vision of God and participation in his divine life. Repetition of the Name of Jesus enhances that longing, again by centering upon what is essential.

In his first Mystical Treatise, Saint Isaac of Nineveh declared,

> The highest degree of silence and inner calmness (*hesychia*) is reached when a person, in the intimate depths of the soul, converses with the divine Presence, and is drawn in spirit to that Presence. When the soul is transfigured by the constant thought of God, with a watchfulness that does

not fade either by day or by night, the Lord sends forth a protecting cloud, that provides shade by day and sheds a radiant light by night. That light shines in the darkness of the soul.

That transfiguring Light is the presence of the Holy Spirit himself, bestowed in baptism, but constantly renewed through the exercise of inner, contemplative prayer. The Prayer of Jesus is a gift, superficially accessible to all, but internalized in the hidden depths of the heart by only a few. If one feels called to pursue 'the hesychast way', it is important to remember that ceaseless prayer must never be sought for its own sake, not even for its perceived spiritual benefits.

Received with thanksgiving as an expression of divine love, the Prayer of Jesus can be offered up as a 'sacrament' of the divine Presence. Through it, 'God is with us,' in an intimate and unique way, to bless, guide, heal and transform the 'secret heart' from stone to flesh and from flesh to spirit. But like every sacramental aspect of life in the Body of Christ, the Prayer can be true to its purpose only insofar as it serves to glorify God and to increase both our faith and our joy in his unfailing presence with us.

RECOMMENDATIONS FOR FURTHER READING

Ignatius Brianchaninov, *On the Prayer of Jesus*. London: Watkins. 1952.

Igumen Chariton of Valamo, *The Art of Prayer*. London: Faber. 1966.

John Climacus [of the ladder], *The Ladder of Divine Ascent*. Translated by Colm Luibhead and Norman Russell. New York: Paulist Press. 1982.

G. E. H. Palmer, Philip Sherrard, Kallistos Ware, edd., *The Philokalia*, 4 volumes to date. London-Boston: Faber. 1979–1996).

Lorenzo Scupoli, Nicodemus of the Holy Mountain, revised by Theophane The Recluse, *Unseen Warfare*. Crestwood, New York: St Vladimir's Seminary Press. 1978.

Benedicta Ward, trans., *The Sayings of the Desert Fathers*. Kalamazoo: Cistercian Publications. 1975.

Kallistos Ware, 'The Jesus Prayer in Saint Gregory of Sinai', *Eastern Churches Review* IV/1 (1972) 3–22.

———. 'Silence in Prayer: The Meaning of Hesychia', in A. M. Allchin (ed.), *Theology and Prayer*, Studies Supplementary to *Sobornost* 3 (London, 1975) 8–28.

———. 'The Spirituality of the Philokalia', *Sobornost* 13/1 (1991) 6–24.

The Way of a Pilgrim and *The Pilgrim Continues His Way*. Translated by R. M. French. 1965. Recently reprinted by Harper Collins, San Francisco. A better translation by Helen Bacovcin has been published by Doubleday Image. New York. 1978.

PIETISM:

The Hymn as Contemplative Prayer

Gustav Kopka, Jr.

WOULD LIKE TO BEGIN with an illumination I had Monday morning in the Cellarium[1] at breakfast. Those beautiful words so loved by Bernard of Clairvaux: 'My beloved is a bundle of myrrh. He shall abide between my breasts.'[2]

It is raining today. That is a blessing, for it should help us focus on the inside, concentrating on the sun of our heart, as those Pietist writers from whom I had so much read to me as a child—Johann Arndt, but also others before him, Thomas à Kempis, Johan Tauler, Martin Luther—liked to talk about the Christian life. It is appropriate to sing a hymn. I am enough of a Lutheran Pietist who thrives on hymn singing to invite you to 'see the doctrines' of such writers in hymn number 356 for example, of The Lutheran Book of Worship: 'O Jesus, Joy of Loving Hearts'. It is one of five hymns in this book attributed to Bernard of Clairvaux, among the many attributed to the pietist mystic tradition. Let us sing all five verses, taking turns between men and women. Extensive hymn singing—at home and in the fields, always singing all the verses—is also part of my Pietist upbringing. Listen to a few brief phrases to start with:

---

1. The basement lounge of the Institute of Cistercian Studies.
2. Song of Songs 1:13.

O Jesus, joy of loving hearts, . . . fount . . . light . . . We taste
you, we taste you, . . . we drink of you . . . For you our
restless spirits yearn . . . your smile . . . O Jesus, . . . shed
o'er the world your holy light.

This topic, Piety and Pietism in the Protestant Tradition, is
a large, broadly sweeping field. It's an elephant! I think I have
hold of something, though I am not quite sure whether it's the
tail or the head. At any rate, I want to share that 'something'
under four sections: First, introductory definitional comments
about myself and Pietism. Second, Martin Luther's piety and its
roots. Third, German Lutheran piety from the late sixteenth
through early eighteenth centuries. Fourth, some pitfalls of
pietism. And all of this, because of the limited time available,
only in the form of *prolegomena*.

PIETISM: A PERSONAL PERSPECTIVE

Through the years, and certainly since my father died, I have
become more interested in trying to understand myself by
understanding him better. He was a pious lay person of a para-
church prayer—preaching—singing fellowship movement, but
a loyal member of the established Evangelical Lutheran Church.
Never did he give us the idea that there was for him hostile
tension between the two. He was not one of those 'Radical
Pietists', as they were later called, (mostly Reformed rather
than Lutheran) who were led to start their own sects or
churches, trying to bring the kingdom of God to this earth
by force. They forgot God's grace and became mostly pre-
occupied with themselves. My father was a pious man who
strongly identified with the school of piety that had come down
through Luther, Arndt, Paul Gerhardt (by many considered
not so much a pietist as an orthodox theologian), and August
Herman Francke. As part of this piety movement we sent a lot
of money to foreign mission societies. Relatives went to serve
in diaconal institutions like Bethel Bielefeld.

Piety! Pietism! What do these words mean? What did it mean to be *pius* in the classical roman society? *Pietas* had to do with a loving loyalty. It did not necessarily mean *Frömmigkeit*, some kind of external or inner religiosity, but had to do with your thoughts, action, and relationship, above all, to your family and, later on, to the state, toward what usually was a benevolent dictator or patriarch.

In classical society, a *templum* was a designated holy space. When I hear the word 'contemplation' I think of a holy space, though not necessarily a place in the geographic sense. Experience repeating itself regularly in some disciplined ways at appointed times, that is what the word contemplation suggests in my spirituality. In the late 1880s, Schleiermacher wrote a three volume book about *Frömmigkeit*, the original German word for what we call piety. He defines it according to his psychology of religion approach as a purely subjective reality, that is, a feeling about one's relation to God. Unfortunately this definition has imprinted itself on the minds of clergy, theological students, and lay people as a *Schwärmer* mentality, an external emotionalism without rationality or discipline. That has been my reading of the word 'piety' in the colloquial usage of the church here in North America. But it is not what German Lutheran Pietism was about. Lutheran piety is focused on submission to the Word of Jesus Christ. And the things that quickly spring to my mind are the things Bernard of Clairvaux mentions in the hymn we just sang. Words like heart, joy, smile, love. Piety has to do with a very intimate, personal way of relating to this Christ. It is the response of the Christian faith to God's address to us, a response of praise, thanksgiving, prayer, and service. What service? Worship service, serving soup, service institutions for the mentally impaired . . . all that and more.

Here the term 'spirituality' might be useful. In some literature it is used almost interchangeably with 'piety'. Early Lutherans, the classic Lutherans, refused to fall off either side of the horse, to paraphrase Luther, that is, the sides of objectivism and subjectivism, individualism and communalism. The people I shall be mentioning today—Arndt, Jakob Boehme, the hymn writers—Philipp Jakob Spener, August Francke—were of that sort. They held both sides in the hands of their heart. However, we must pay attention to what they were addressing at a particular point of their writing. If they are discussing the stultifying of faith by super-orthodox objectifying, then they may sound like *Schwärmer*, enthusiasts.

Sacramentum Mundi contains a good introductory paragraph on Pietism by Wenzel Lohff:

> Pietism is a comprehensive term for a widespread and manifold movement within Protestantism in the early seventeenth century. The first half of the eighteenth century was its heyday but it made itself felt in the nineteenth century revivalism and is still a force even today (e.g. among the Moravian Brethren and some types of Methodism). Pietism does not look on the Reformation as a mere occurrence in the past that is now embodied in an institution, but as an event that the Church must constantly actualize if Christ's kingdom is to be a living reality. The substance of all pietism is a longing for *praxis pietatis*, the exercise of godliness. For pietism, the real purpose of redemption is to bring the religious subjectivity of man into lively, spontaneous play, and such is also the main interest in theology. There is no difficulty in the old-established Protestant denominations about stressing a subjective approach, but radical pietism has the effect of loosening Church bonds.'[3]

I am pleased with this introduction to an extensive article in this roman catholic resource.

'A wandering European was my father.' That different hearing of the Genesis verse has become a key phrase in my self-understanding as a classic Lutheran Pietist. My father's 'wanderings', path, way, contemplation—from East to West

---

3. Karl Rahner et al. *Sacramentum Mundi*. Six vols. (New York: Herder and Herder. 1968–1970) Here, volume 5, page 24.

and back again, as a political draftee as well as through the broad spiritual riches of Christianity—helps me to understand what it means to be a Pietist. For example, the earthy, common spirituality experienced among the slavic Orthodox as well as Roman Catholic; the singing of hymns as a form of non-violent witness against communism or earlier Nazi oppression; listening to political speeches, then walking away; working in the field, mixing in the crowds of the town, at school, humming, singing a hymn, only to be sat upon by teachers. These pictures came back up in my mind when I was in the German Democratic Republic, the Soviet Union, and other eastern european countries in the seventies and eighties.

German pietism, German Lutheran pietism, has a clear understanding of objective truth, raised and based on Catechism, Confessions and traditional liturgy, and senses what is between the lines in the spiritual poetry of the hymns and the prayers. Here again the Lutheran part includes much that has existed before and since Martin Luther—as sayings which I have copied down over the years will show.

> Ah, Lord God, thou holy lover of my soul, when thou comest into my soul, all that is within me shall rejoice. Thou art my glory, and the exultation of my heart; thou art my hope and refuge in the day of trouble. Set me free from all evil passions, and heal my heart of all inordinate affections; that being inwardly cured and thoroughly cleansed, I may be made fit to love, courageous to suffer, steady to persevere. Nothing is sweeter than love . . .
>
> *Thomas à Kempis*

> O thou loving and tender Father in heaven, we confess before thee in sorrow how hard and unsympathetic are our hearts; . . . O Father, forgive this our sin, and lay it not to our charge. Give us grace ever to alleviate the crosses and difficulties of those around us, and never add to them; teach us to be consolers in sorrow, to take thought for the stranger, the widow, and the orphan; let our charity show itself, not in words only, but in deed and truth. Teach us to

judge as thou dost, with forbearance, with much pity and indulgence; help us to avoid all unloving judgment of others; for the sake of Jesus thy Son, who loved us and gave himself for us.

Johann Arndt

Almighty Father, enter thou our hearts and so fill us with thy love, that forsaking all evil desires, we may embrace thee, our only good. Show unto us, for thy mercy's sake, O Lord our God, what thou art unto us. Say unto our souls, "I am thy salvation." So speak that we may hear. Our hearts are before thee; open thou our ears; let us hasten after thy voice, and take hold on thee. Hide not thy face from us, we beseech thee, O Lord. Enlarge thou the narrowness of our souls, that thou mayest enter in. Repair the ruinous mansions, that thou mayest dwell there.

Saint Augustine

'Christ for us.' 'Christ in us'. These are two key phrases from Martin Luther. But most lutheran theologians have ignored the mystic affinity he intended.

Heiko Oberman of Tübingen wrote in his preface to Johann Arndt's *True Christianity* in the Classics of Western Spirituality series[4] that Arndt was

an observant reader and perceptive student of Martin Luther's work . . . Arndt discerned behind the theological conclusions of Luther the function of true doctrine as the perimeter around the experience of penance and salvation; in short, he brought to light again the spontaneity of Christian service as the true fruit of a living faith.[5]

Arndt saw, underscored, and applied

Luther's vision that justification by faith alone does not preclude but, to the contrary, unleashes good works in terms of the whole Christian, his action in the Church and in the world.

4. Johann Arndt, *True Christianity* (New York: Paulist Press, 1979).

5. *Ibid.*, xv.

Long before scholars decreed the mutual exclusion between 'Reformation' and 'mysticism', Luther himself had in-
gested and incorporated into his own thinking the sermons
of Bernard of Clairvaux (+1153), the biblical piety of his
spiritual director Johannes Staupitz (+1525) and the meditations of Johannes Tauber (+1361). The inner suspense
and the dynamic contrast between the pains of desolation
and the excesses of joy in the experience of untrammeled
faith characterize his spirituality, just as the famous formula
'righteous and sinner at once' (simul justus et peccator)
catches the exact paradox of his doctrine of justification.[6]

Oberman adds: 'In this respect Arndt is a second Luther'.

In 1976 Professor Bengt Hoffman, Professor of Ethics and
Ecumenics at Gettysburg Seminary, published his Luther and the
Mystics.[7] While it is true that Luther rejected all schemes of
salvation, mystical or otherwise, that did not have Christ at the
center, and insisted that the Gospel be anchored in history and
Scripture, he did not neglect the personal, non-rational aspects
of faith. Luther spoke of 'the Kingdom within us' and of our
'mystical union' with Christ. He had a lifelong appreciation of
Bernard of Clairvaux, Tauler, the unknown author of Theologica
Germanica, and others.

> O love, holy and chaste! O sweet and gracious affection! O
> pure and refined intent of the will, all the more pure and
> refined because in it remains no trace of itself, all the more
> gracious and sweet because what is felt is solely divine. So
> to be moved is to be deified.[8]
> So prayed Bernard of Clairvaux. He also said: 'Through
> Christ your sins are forgiven. This is the testimony the Holy
> Spirit has put into your heart . . . by the death of the Only-
> begotten we obtain that we have been justified freely by

6. Ibid.
7. Bengt R. Hoffman. Luther and the Mystics (Minneapolis: Augsburg, 1976).
8. Quoting Bernard of Clairvaux, De diligendo Deo. Cambridge Patristic Texts
(Cambridge, 1926) Chapter 10.

His blood, the forgiveness of sins, according to the riches of his grace.'[9]

Meister Eckhart speaks of detachment, *Abgeschiedenheit,* when he says that 'the spirit should be immovable before all the vicissitudes of love and suffering, honor, disgrace and shame, like a mountain of lead against a breeze. This immovable detachment brings men into the greatest likeness with God because the fact that God is God comes from his immovable detachment. . . . He who would attain perfect detachment must seek perfect humility by which he may come to the closest proximity to the Godhead.'[10]

Luther also appreciated Tauler's insights about the joy-filled presence, the nearness of God. 'A pure heart is more precious in the sight of God than ought else on earth. A pure heart is . . . a treasury of divine riches, a storehouse of divine sweetness, the reward of all the life and sufferings of Christ.'[11] And with Thomas à Kempis (1379/80–1473), Luther 'would rather feel compunction than to know its definition. . . . A humble acquaintance with one self is a more certain way to God than a profound inquiry after knowledge.'[12]

Though in the later Middle Ages scholastic theology and piety—often in the form of mysticism—went their separate ways, it is a unique characteristic of Luther's theology that these two are reconciled and organically interwoven. Hoffman argues that 'Martin Luther's faith-consciousness was significantly molded by mystical experience and that western de-

---

9. E. G. Schwiebert, quoting Bernard of Clairvaux in *Luther and His Times* (St Louis: Concordia, 1950) 171.

10. Eduard Schaefer, *Meister Eckharts Traktat 'Von Abgeschiedenlheit'* (Bonn, 1956) 214–217.

11. Susanna Winkworth, translator, *The History of John Tauler* (New York, 1858). Excerpts from The Cologne edition of Tauler's Sermons, 1543.

12. Thomas à Kempis, *The Imitation of Christ,* Opera Omnia I-II, ed. M. I. Pohl (Freiburg im Br., 1910).

pendence on rationalism has obscured or eclipsed this mystical light'.[13]

In his concluding chapter Hoffman points to a traditional lack in Christian theology, namely, the

> inability to deal with the Third Article of the Creed. Theology has always found it hard to annotate in integral fashion the stirring of the Holy Spirit in a Christian way and view of life. It registers admirably the historical and phenomenological data of revelation, whether the revelation is considered a once-for-all event or regarded as an ongoing process. But what can a linear and logical mind do with a wind which bloweth whither it listeth or a Lord who pledges that he will be present after his death wherever two or three are gathered in his name or that his Spirit will, through his followers, do greater things than he did?[14]

This is a challenge to Lutherans through the centuries and to Protestantism in general.

What about the doing of faith? Most frequently Lutherans have been relegated to the quietistic camp. Allegedly, a mystic is by definition a non-doer. It has been part of my own formation as a Lutheran Pietist that this is not so. 'Even a cursory glance at the history of Lutheran pietism' writes Hoffman, 'should correct the error. Most missionary undertakings, issuing from the "pietistic" experience of God's gracious presence, also disprove the long-lived fallacy'.[15]

> Martin Luther spoke of moral fruits growing out of the justified life. . . . the Christian is a transmitter of moral force from God, we read in Luther's comments on Galatians. This force is no less potent because it is invisible. . . . The meditations and supplications of a person in communion with God are so essential that . . . the world would indeed

13. Hoffman, p. 18.
14. *Ibid.*, 217.
15. *Ibid.*, 232–233.

be unprotected without the hidden life of Christians in the mystical Christ.[16]

Luther was indeed 'a crystal with many facets'. Above all, he was 'a person of spirituality, living in Christ, yearning for Christ's entry into the soul, knowing about God's presence, experiencing healing grace'.[17] Luther's piety was rooted in the concepts of justification, sanctification, and faith. Justification includes new birth and new obedience, new freedom, a joyful trust and a solid assurance of belonging to the community, the body of Christ. Sanctification is never something other than a new beginning. Everything depends on the grace of God. Faith/trust (*Glaube*) is the only way. 'Glaubst du, so hast du' Luther writes in his essay on *Christian Freedom*. Progress in faith, love, and good works, in spirituality/piety is always a beginning. It is not an increasing quality of life but an expanding submission into the merciful hands of God. 'Fortschreiten heißt, immer von Neuem beginnen!' In Latin: '*Proficere hoc est semper a novo incipere!*' This progress cannot be measured by psychological criteria. It is not an evolution.

THE FOUNDERS OF GERMAN LUTHERAN PIETISM

Three representative early founders of German Lutheran Pietism, among many others, are Johann Arndt, Jakob Boehme, and Paul Gerhardt.

Many call Johann Arndt (1555–1620) the 'Father of German Piety'. Albert Schweitzer—who gained from his mother a love for Arndt—at the age of eighty-three in 1955, the four-hundredth anniversary of Arndt's birth, wrote: 'He was a prophet of interior Protestantism', but a prophet with little following in the twentieth century. In the 1880's Albrecht

16. *Ibid.*, 235–236.
17. *Ibid.*, 236.

Ritschl published his three volume *History of Pietism*[18] and established a strong antagonism to mystical writing and pietism of the Arndt-Spener-Francke type. Karl Barth continued this antagonism. So did others.

Lutheran orthodoxy dominated the seventeenth and early eighteenth centuries. It opposed those primarily interested in the practice of piety with their emphasis on renewal, individual growth in holiness, and religious experience. Johann Arndt became a spokesman for the *praxis* of piety, the practice of the Christian life. A pastor who stuck to his guns, he moved more often than the average parish clergyman, not by his own choice. He edited Luther's edition of *Theologia Germanica* as well as *Imitatio Christi* by à Kempis. Several of his own works on spirituality followed. In 1610 his four books on *True Christianity* were published, and before his death eleven years later, had gone through twenty editions. Two books were added later.

Arndt's Foreword is addressed 'To The Christian Reader'. In it Arndt decries the 'great and shameful abuse' of his day:

> Such ungodly conduct gave me cause to write this book to show simple readers wherein true Christianity consists, namely, in the exhibition of a true, living faith, active in Christ, not only because we ought to believe in Christ, but also because we are to live in Christ and he in us. . . . Adam must die, and Christ must live, in us. It is not enough to know God's word: one must also practise it in a living, active manner. . . . Everyone wishes very much to be servant of Christ, but no one wishes to be his follower. . . . It is now the desire of the world to know all things, but that which is better than all knowledge, namely, 'to know the love of Christ' (Eph 3:19), no one desires to learn. No one can love Christ who does not follow the example of his holy life. . . . True Christianity consists, not in words or in external show,

18. Bonn, 1880–1886; Reprinted Berlin, 1966. See the discussion in Oberman and Hoffmann.

but in living faith, from which arise righteous fruits, and all manner of Christian virtues, as from Christ himself. Since faith is hidden from human eyes and is invisible, it must be manifested by its fruits, inasmuch as faith creates from Christ all that is good, righteous and holy.[19]

Arndt acknowledges that he is basing much of what he has to say on Tauler, à Kempis and others 'who may seem to ascribe more than is due to human ability and works'.[20] But he reminds 'the Christian reader that he continually look to the great object and purpose for which [he] wrote this book'.[21]

In Book I Arndt develops fifteen 'beautiful rules for a Christian life', beginning with this one:

> If you are not able to practice a perfect life as is commanded in God's word and as you very much would like to, you are nevertheless to wish [to practice this life]. Such holy desires are truly pleasant to God and God accepts them as acts, for he looks on the heart and not on the works. Nevertheless, at all times you are to mortify your flesh and not allow it to rule.

And in rule six:

> If God gives you heavenly consolation and joy, accept it with humble thanks. If God, however, takes away his consolation, know that this is a mortification of the flesh and is better than the joy of the spirit. Pain and suffering make a sinful man much healthier than do joy and happiness. Many of you come by too great spiritual joy into pride.[22]

In Book VI, a brief 'Second Essay to All Lovers of True Godliness, dedicated to the mayor and council of the city of Danzig on June 10, 1620,' Arndt states:

19. *True Christianity*, 21–23.
20. *Ibid.*, 25.
21. *Ibid.*, 25.
22. *Ibid.*, 178–179.

Many a man thinks he truly knows Christ if he can dispute much about the person of Christ. Yet if he does not live in Christ, he deceives himself. The person who does not have Christ's humility, patience, and meekness in his heart, and does not experience it, does not know Christ nor does he have him in a proper fashion nor does he taste him properly, and he who preaches the doctrine of Christ and does not follow his noble life preaches but only half of Christ.[23]

And later:

Christ and faith are so united with one another that everything that is Christ is ours through faith. Where Christ lives through faith, there he brings about a holy life and that is the noble life of Christ in us. Where Christ's life is, there is pure love; and where love is, there is the Holy Spirit; and where the Holy Spirit is, there is the whole kingdom of God. If a man has one thing he has everything, but if he does not have one thing he has nothing. If he does not have from Christ a holy, noble, and new life, he has nothing from Christ, from faith, from the new birth.[24]

Jacob Boehme (1575–1624) layman, shoemaker, businessman, struggled with the ugly violence of his day, the Thirty Years War (1618–1648). During the last four years of his life he wrote *The Way to Christ*.[25] Professor Winfried Zeller of Marburg writes in the Preface to the modern translation:

Contemporary man, as well, so easily given to thoughtlessness and superficiality, can learn from Jacob Boehme's profound spirituality. Our age, which suffers in a purely external, material mode of thought, is at the same time filled with a deep longing for authentic interiority. The modern orientation to mystical reflection on the self arises in no way from an introverted egoism. The man of the present longs from the depths of his being to gain inner unification in face

23. *Ibid.*, 27.
24. *Ibid.*, 278.
25. Jacob Boehme. *The Way to Christ* (New York: Paulist Press, 1978).

of manifold distraction and to find the central and essential
in face of the peripheral and extraneous. . . . Boehme can
offer significant spiritual aid. As his book *The Way to Christ*
indicates, Christian piety begins with repentance, that is,
with self-understanding in which man comes to know the
unfathomable self-seeking at the base of his being. . . . From
Boehme one can learn the decisive step from meditative
religiosity to spiritual worship.[26]

Zeller concludes:

All unrest in the world is caused by the inner anxiety of man.
Boehme agrees with Augustine that only the man who has
found peace of heart in God is able to bring the world to
peace. In the soul of man himself lies the basis of his feeling
of misfortune. Deep in his interior dwell melancholy and
dread. . . . In spite of the narrowness of this environment,
Jacob Boehme was a man of universal spirit.[27]

Paul Tillich wrote in a brief Foreword to John Stoudt's
biography of Boehme:[28]

Although Boehme's thoughts have changed during his writings from a stage of crudity to a stage of comparative clarity
they are always expressed in a language which mirrors
speculative vision, mystical experience, psychological insight,
and alchemist traditions. It is often difficult to uncover the rational element in this mixture, but it is there . . . If Protestant
theology wants to penetrate the ontological implications of
the Christian symbols, it would do well to use the ideas of
Boehme more than those of Aristotle.[29]

Jacob Boehme provides 'one of the most profound and
strangest systems of Western thought'.[30]

---

26. *The Way to Christ*, Introduction, p. xiii.
27. *Ibid.*, p. xv.
28. John Joseph Stoudt. *Jacob Boehme: His Life and Thought* (New York: Seabury,
1968).
29. *Ibid.*, 7.
30. *Ibid.*, 8.

When in the struggle between equally stubborn parties 'creed followed creed, book answered book, dispute succeeded dispute'[31] writes Stoudt, 'Jacob Boehme's religious knowledge began in mystical vision and realized itself in mature rational expression through living. . . . Slowly, as he matured, vision and life were fused . . .' In that, states Stoudt, Boehme 'both reflected and transcended his age'.[32]

We read in Boehme's *Short Form of confession before the Eyes of God*:

> O great, unsearchable, holy God, Lord of all being, who in Christ Jesus, out of pure love for us, revealed your holy being in our humanity, I, a poor, unworthy, sinful man, come before your revealed face, in the humanity of Jesus Christ . . . O God in Christ Jesus, who for the sake of poor sinners became man so that you may help them, to you I cry: I still have a spark of refuge for you in my soul. . . . O merciful God, it is because of your love and patience that I am not already lying in hell. I give myself up with my whole will, thought and mind to your grace, and ask for your mercy. . . . O great foundation of the love of God, . . . O breath of the great love of God, revive my weak breath in me so that it may begin to hunger and thirst after you. . . . O deepest love of all, take my soul's desire into you . . . O God, Holy Spirit, my savior in Christ, teach me what I ought to do so that I might turn to you. Redirect my will in me to you. . . . O God in Christ Jesus, I am blind to myself. . . . I lie before you as a dead man whose life, like a small spark, hovers at his lips. Ignite it, Lord. Direct my soul's breath to you. Lord, I wait on your promise . . . I sink myself into the death of my savior Jesus Christ. . . . [33]

Boehme's guide as to *How the soul ought to meet its dear lover when he knocks in the centrum in the locked room of the soul*:

31. *Ibid.*, 33.
32. *Ibid.*, 41.
33. Boehme, 34–37.

Dear Soul, you must always be in earnest, without relenting. You will obtain the love of a kiss from the noble Sophia in the holy name of Jesus for she stands immediately before the soul's door and knocks and warns the sinner of godless ways. If he desires her love she is willing and kisses him with a beam of her sweet love, by which the heart receives joy. But she does not immediately enter the marriage bed with the soul. . . . [34]

Another *Short Formula of Prayer* 'when the noble Sophia kisses the soul with her love and offers love to it' contains the lines: 'O holiest and deepest love of God in Christ Jesus, give me your pearl, press it into my soul. Take my soul into your arms. O sweetest love, . . . O Highest love, . . . O mighty love, . . .'.[35]

In 1624 Boehme wrote *The Third Treatise on Holy Prayer With an Order for Each Day of the Week.* His introduction reads:

How a man is continually to examine the office, position and way of life in which God has placed him; and how he is to commit the beginning, middle and end of all his activities to God and continually do all his works with God even as the branch of a tree bears its twigs by the power of the root and from these bears its fruit; and how in all his beginnings he is to fetch the power for his works from God's fountain and thank his creator for all blessings.

Together with a heartfelt consideration of the suffering, death and resurrection of Jesus Christ; how a man is continually to lead his soul's hunger and desire through Christ's death into his resurrection in God and press forward to the new birth so that he might pray in spirit and in truth and present himself before God. Written at the request and desires of his dear and good friends for the daily practice of true Christianity in their heart and house-churches.[36]

34. *Ibid.,* 43–44.
35. *Ibid.,* 49.
36. *Ibid.,* 71.

Let me add, finally, these words from Stoudt's Epilogue:

Jacob Boehme had seen eternity's dawn. . . . As his follower, poet Angelus Silesius, wrote: 'Jesu, ew'ge Sonne,/Aller Engel Wonne,/Was für Freude muß es sein/Wenn du kommst ins Herz hinein.' . . . Boehme—and now, perhaps, we may want to call him the 'blessed Jacob'—was a Christian mystic on whom the gracious Spirit had descended. . . . he stood in the line of the prophets who, without benefit of priestly ordination, had seen the mystery unfold itself. . . . he had climbed no ladders . . . God had come down to him. Thus did he reject classical mysticism's ascending Gothic, the mysticism of hierarchies, fashioning instead a properly Protestant mystical genre of descending Agape. He wanted nothing of ladders, pilgrimages, levels, stages degrees, hierarchies— the ascending steps of an ambitious faith seeking to seize and to know the Godhead. For between medieval mysticism and Boehme there towered Luther and his simul justus et peccator, for the reformer had centered the attention on the psychology rather than the mechanics of repentance. . . . This mystical revolution—and that is what it really was— was wrought when Boehme, freed from a medievalism which had been shackled by Greek metaphysics, sought to combine the new cosmology of the Renaissance with his Lutheran Bible.[37]

Paul Gerhardt (1606–1676) poet and pastor, has been called 'the greatest hymn writer after Luther', 'the foremost of German hymn writers', one 'greater even than Luther', 'the most gifted author of religious songs whom the German church has ever known', 'the Asaph of the Lutheran Church'.[38] Like the hymns of Luther, Gerhardt's were sung not only in church but also in homes, shops and marketplace, even by armies on the march. They continue to be soul music to a strong streak of Lutheran piety.

37. Ibid., 299–302.
38. C. George Fry, Paul Gerhardt, Poet and Pastor, The Bride of Christ, vol. 11, no. 4, p. 32.

In a vocational crisis which formed part of a major mid-life trauma, Gerhardt turned at the age of fifty-nine from the tragedies of his century and of his family to an ever deeper faith. He expressed that profoundly positive faith in one hundred-thirty-four german and fourteen latin hymns. Of these at least thirty have become 'classics' of contemporary Christianity. *The Lutheran Book of Worship* includes ten.

> O Lord, how shall I meet you,
> How welcome you aright? . . .
> My hope, my heart's delight!
> Oh, kindle, Lord most holy,
> Your lamp within my breast
> To do in spirit lowly
> All that may please you best.
>
> My heart shall bloom forever . . .
> Oh, love beyond all telling,
> That led you to embrace
> In love, all love excelling,
> Our lost and fallen race.

Or:

> A lamb goes uncomplaining forth . . .
> This lamb is Christ, our greatest friend . . .
> He answered from his tender heart . . .
> His love is dress enough for me . . .
> His Church, the well appointed bride.

Or:

> Christ, the sun of gladness,
> Dispelling all our sadness,
> Shines down on us in warmest light.

Or, my favorite childhood verse of his long evening hymn:

> Breit aus die Flugel beide,
> O Jesu, meine Freude,
> und nimm dein Kuchlein ein.
> Will Satan mich verschlingen,

so lass die Englein singen:
'Dies Kind soll unverletzet sein!

Lord Jesus, since you love me,
Now spread your wings above me
And shield me from alarm.
Though evil would assail me,
Your mercy will not fail me;
I rest in your protecting arm.

Also:

Jesus, thy boundless love to me . . . be thou alone my constant flame.

And:

If God himself be for me . . . For joy my heart is ringing, all sorrow disappears.

And so on.

C. George Fry writes: 'The hymns of Paul Gerhardt speak to the entire life of Catholic faith.'[39]

They deal with adoration, changing seasons, night and day, and the nations, as well as being outpourings of personal love for the Savior Christ. One musical historian claims that Gerhardt 'perfectly combines the objectivity of Orthodoxy, the subjectivity of Pietism'.[40] Fry concludes:

The heart of Gerhardt's hymnody, however, is found in the proclamation and the celebration of the central mysteries of the Catholic faith. His poetry often follows the church year . . . Gerhardt disproves the criticism that 'Lutheran Orthodoxy was obsessed with death' by his balanced treatment of 'the living Christ in the Church today.' . . . Gerhardt drew heavily on the Scriptures, especially the Psalter . . . and the Gospels. Next to the Canon Gerhardt relied on

39. *Ibid.*, 33.
40. *Ibid.*, 33.

the Latin heritage of piety, especially the theologians and
poets of the High Middle Ages. This was supplemented by
his observations of nature, his reflections on the spiritual life,
and his experiences as a pastor and priest. Binding all these
ingredients together was an immersion in the Lutheran
ethos as known in both the Confessions and in the writings
of the Reformer.

His hymns have challenged the imagination of English-language
translators and in many denominations he is recognized as
a churchly, sacramental, evangelical, and Catholic churchman
within the Lutheran tradition.

Peter Erb, who teaches English and Religion and Culture
at Wilfrid Laurier University, Waterloo, Ontario, is the editor
of *Pietists, Selected Writings*. 'Pietism,' he claims in his opening
sentence of the Foreword, 'was the most important development in Protestant spirituality.'[41] E. Ernest Stoeffler, Professor Emeritus of Religion at Temple University and writer of
significant volumes on Evangelical, German, and Continental
Pietism, adds: 'Pietism is today considered to have been one
of the most influential Protestant reform movements since the
Reformation itself.' Yet only marginal attention has been paid to
it by historians or it has been totally ignored. That situation has
changed since the mid-sixties, however. The renewed interest
in and expansion of hymnody, individual and family prayer,
worship and Bible study as well as the renewal of a sense of
vocation are only some of the recent experiences that exhibit
various similarities with the concerns of early Pietists.

Erb is right when he states that,

> the beginning of the movement itself can be located and
> dated with precision. In 1675 Philipp Jakob Spener, se-
> nior pastor of the Frankfurt am Main ministerium, wrote
> a preface to the postills of Johann Arndt. He entitled the
> piece *Pia Desideria* (*Pious Desires*) and in it he advocated a

41. Peter Erb, Foreword. *Pietists, Selected Writings* (New York: Paulist Press, 1983)
xv-xvi.

renewed emphasis on biblical preaching and on the experience of repentance and the new birth, the establishment of
conventicles for the mutual edification and admonition of
the 'reborn' believers, and a reform of pastoral training that
would place less emphasis on scholastic polemical theology
and more on the development of a sensitized ministry
concerned with the practical devotional and moral life of
parishioners.

Spener's *Pia Desideria* was immediately popular and by
the close of the century its principles had affected all Ger-
man-speaking Protestant communities in Europe and America. Under Spener's protege, August Hermann Francke, the
Pietist interest in ecumenism, missions, social service, and
lay and pastoral education was furthered at the university
of Halle (a.S.). . . . In both its churchly and radical forms
the influence of Pietism was great. Without it, it is difficult
to understand the growth of 'evangelical' Christianity in
Europe and America, and its adherents played central roles
in the development of Protestant hymnological, devotional,
theological, and biblical studies.[42]

Although formally Protestant Pietism must pay extensive
and thorough attention to this Spener-Francke-Halle school
of pietism, a further treatment of it would go far beyond the
limited scope of a German Lutheran Pietism rooted in Luther,
pre-reformation mystics, Boehme, Arndt, and the many hymn
writers—especially when one considers the overall umbrella
of this workshop, 'The Contemplative Way: Recovering a Lost
Tradition'. Suffice it to say that German Lutheran Pietists, as I
have experienced its spiritual formation on the Continent and
in later academic reflection and pastoral-ecclesial pervasion in
the United States, is intensely personal and at the same time
focused on objective and communal spirituality. A repentant
heart and personal confession of sins leads to an intimate experience of the grace of God. Humble belief in the all-gracious
God was in Luther's theology the only possible expression
of piety.

42. *Ibid.*, 33–34.

PITFALLS OF PIETISM

The norwegian theologian Andreas Aarflot, in his discussion of the types of lutheran piety[43] reminds us that 'usually the institutional aspects of the church or the influential personalities get more attention than the hidden streams which carry the life of the faithful in the church.'[44] Consequently it is difficult to trace or to analyze piety. There is a distinct lack of what scholars call reliable source material about what was actually believed by pietists. 'The inner life of a church, as it is expressed in the spirituality of its members, is seldom accessible to objective analysis.'[45] Nevertheless, there are clues in letters, autobiographies, devotional books, prayers, and hymns.

For Lutherans, as for early Christians, early intentions soon took a different direction in church life from that first envisioned. Early Lutherans were against starting a new church. They emphasized the catholicity of the evangelical faith. Reception of ancient creeds was crucial, and the Confessions had a position subordinate to Scripture.

Pietism was concerned about the individual believer and his personal relationship to God. It was a matter of the heart. Experience of salvation occurred independent of membership in the church. But what soon became important was the gathering of the witnessing faithful which sometimes, as in the case of the radical Pietists, led to separation. Confessional, denominational structures were unimportant. In Scandinavia, pious lay preachers were often opposed by the clergy.

According to Luther, it is of the essence of piety to stand in close relation to the Christian Church, the *praxis* of faith and life which grows from the sacramental community. For Luther

43. Andreas Aarflot, *Typen Lutherischer Frömmigkeit*, ed. Vilmos Vajta, Die Kirchen des Welt, Band 15 (Evangelisches Verlagswerk, 1977) pp. 161–179.

44. *Ibid.*, 161.

45. *Ibid.*

this included the daily life of one's vocation. In this connection Luther became very critical of the monastic life as some ideal form of spirituality.

There were new tendencies in post-reformation piety. For Luther confession included repentance and faith. Melanchthon and others added the new obedience. For Luther sanctification was part of justification. Later Lutherans differentiated more strictly between the two. There was an attempt to identify psychologically steps in the development of the Christian life, leading to the concept of an inner *unio mystica* not dissimilar from medieval Roman Catholic mysticism. Signs of this can be found in Arndt and in hymns of the mid-sixteenth to mid-seventeenth century. In *True Christianity* we see a tendency towards understanding grace as the efficacious power of the spirit rather than as God's favor. Paul Gerhardt, in some hymns, sings of the new human nature, which suggests that being close to God is the highest level of blessedness. In fact, Lutheran Orthodoxy tended to speak of sanctification as progressive improvement of one's relationship to God.

The pietistic movement from 1675 to 1750 tended toward individualism, utopianism, and trust in human possibilities. As such, it tended to emphasize the person justified rather than the justifying grace of God, the subjective working out of salvation in the individual life rather than the objective reality of God's work of salvation, and the communion of saints as a group of new-way individuals who had had similar experiences.

A negative attitude toward the world as the home of a corrupted humanity tended to lead to a new legalism, even while it advanced what Spener called a 'hope for better times'.

The concept of change in society through change of the individual led to the establishment of social and educational institutions. Yet the basic lutheran theology of the world as God's good creation and of ministry in daily life to the glory of God as the true shape of piety tended to get left out in later pietism.

To summarize let me use three headings:

(1) A distortion of lutheran objectivism: Luther's statement that 'I believe that I cannot by my own reason or strength'[46] or emotional intimacy or whatever 'come to the Lord Jesus Christ'. That is 'Christ For Us'. Pietism tends to replace this with an exclusive 'Christ In Us'. Some lutheran theologians would call this a psychological, anthropological phenomenon and not a matter of faith.

(2) A negation of the church visible and institutional as the body of Christ. The church's earthliness, yes, earthiness, is rejected as evil. In other words, because the church is in the world it is judged to be automatically of the world. The intention— obsession?—to conquer this big bad world and take it over denies the truth that this world is God's creation.

(3) The view of daily life as utilitarian rather than sacramental. The danish lutheran pietistic theologian Pontoppidan put it this way in his 1737 *Explanation* of Luther's *Small Catechism*: 'Dear Child, would you like to be happy on earth and finally be saved in heaven?' The anticipated answer, no doubt, is: 'I sure would'. This emphasis on happiness is a far cry from the concept of service in lutheran piety. 'Faith active in love', to quote Luther, is the free, grateful response of the believer to God's graceful kindness and mercy.

I want to close this brief treatment of the pitfalls of pietism with these words from Bengt Hoffman:[47]

> Experiential piety has of course sometimes turned into le-
> galism. But we tend to toss out the baby with the bath water
> by speaking perjoratively of piety-grounded religion. . . . let
> us not forget that no faith and no true Christian ethics
> exists without a measure of prayer-borne spirituality, i.e.

46. Luther's Explanation to the Third Article of the Apostles Creed in the *Small Catechism*.

47. Hoffman, pp. 218–219.

piety. Arndt, Spener and Francke—persons of piety in the history of Lutheranism—correctly counted themselves partakers of the kind of experienced grace which Luther had called *sapientia experimentalis*. Their piety and the piety of many later Lutheran 'pietists' lie within, not outside, Luther's perception of faith.

CONCLUSION

On the wintry December day of the Holy Innocents, Martyrs, *Anno Domini* 1987, Joseph Sittler died. He was and continues to be my american model for doing Religion and Cultural Theology as a german lutheran Pietist. At the funeral service of this doxologically passionate, profoundly paradoxical, and poetically pious man of God, the assembled congregation sang as the main hymn one selected for this occasion by 'Joe' himself: 'Herzlich lieb hab ich dich, O Herr.' Martin Schalling (1532–1608), a favorite student of Martin Luther's theological research assistant at Wittenberg University, Philipp Melanchthon, wrote the hymn while facing societal turmoil, professional ministry insecurities, and approaching blindness. Catherine Winkworth, that nineteenth-century piously prayerful and poetically potent british intellect, translated it and many other sixteenth- to eighteenth-century german hymns into English. I quote the entire hymn, three long verses, as a bond with those before me, as an almost daily prayer of my calling to be, and as a hopeful gift to those in my extended family of blood and marriage as well as of the entire *oikumene*. May they continue the tradition of 'heart, mind and soul' with their 'hearts and hands and voices'.

> Lord, thee I love with all my heart;
> I pray thee, ne'r from me depart;
> With tender mercy cheer me.
> Earth has no pleasure I would share,
> Yea, heav'n itself were void and bare
> If thou, Lord, wert not near me.

And should my heart for sorrow break,
My trust in thee can nothing shake.
Thou art the portion I have sought;
Thy precious blood my soul has bought.
Lord Jesus Christ, My God and Lord, my God and Lord,
Forsake me not! I trust thy Word.

Yea, Lord, 'twas thy rich bounty gave
My body, soul and all I have
In this poor life of labor.
Lord, grant that I in ev'ry place
May glorify thy lavish grace
And serve and help my neighbor.
Let no false doctrine me beguile
Let Satan not my soul defile.
Give strength and patience unto me
To bear my cross and follow thee.
Lord Jesus Christ, My God and Lord, my God and Lord,
In death thy comfort still afford.

Lord, let at last thine angels come,
To Abr'ham' bosom bear me home,
That I may die unfearing;
And in its narrow chamber keep
My body safe in peaceful sleep
Until thy reappearing.
And then from death awaken me,
That these mine eyes with joy may see,
O Son of God, thy glorious face,
My Savior and my fount of grace.
Lord Jesus Christ, My prayer attend, my prayer attend,
And I will praise thee without end.[48]

48. Hymn 325 in *The Lutheran Book of Worship* (Minneapolis: Augsburg Press, 1978).

RECOMMENDATIONS FOR FURTHER READING

The Imitation of Christ, edited by Harold C. Gardiner, sj. New York: Doubleday Image. 1955, 1959. (There are numerous editions in print.)

Johann Arndt: True Christianity, Peter C. Erb, ed. New York: Paulist Press. 1979.

Jacob Boehme: The Way to Christ. Peter C. Erb, ed. New York: Paulist Press. 1978.

John and Charles Wesley. Selected Prayers, Hymns, Journal, Notes, Letters, and Treatises. Frank Whaling, ed. New York: Paulist Press. 1981.

Pietists. Selected Writings. Peter C. Erb, ed. New York: Paulist Press. 1983.

Philip Jakob Spener, *Pia Desideria*. Philadelphia, Fortress Press. 1964.

The Theologia Germanica of Martin Luther, translated by Bengt Hoffmann. New York: Paulist Press. 1980.

William Law: A Serious Call to Devout and Holy Life, and The Spirit of Love. New York: Paulist Press. 1978.

WORD AND WORK

Praying with Mind and Body

GilChrist Lavigne, OCSO

YOU MAY HAVE HEARD that for a monk or nun living the Rule of Benedict, the day is typically divided into periods for prayer, reading and work. A typically bene-dictine motto is *Ora et labora*: 'Pray and work'. Father Basil Pennington writes about Centering Prayer, an avenue to prayer that has become very important to him and to many other people. I will describe two other monastic forms of prayer: *lectio divina* (holy reading) and work. But when both Basil and I have finished, I hope you will see that all these activities—prayer, reading, work—form a unity in the *Rule of Benedict* and in a monastic house. Even though there may be specific hours of the day that seem dedicated more to one aspect than another, often in the heart of the monk or nun all of them are going on at once. Prayer becomes a fabric of life. It goes on unceasingly in the background all through the day. Holy reading or *lectio divina* is an approach to reading which leads a person into prayer and contemplation. While there is often a feeling in many monasteries that 'real *lectio*' (and I put those words in quotation marks) is done only with the Sacred Scriptures, yet, if this holy reading, this *lectio*, is genuine, it becomes a habit and a way that spills into all life. It becomes an attitude and a posture, a stance that one takes towards everyone, everything, every moment of the day. Work is also completely intermingled in this reality. Work—whether manual labor (the traditional work of monks and nuns) or scholarly or administrative or people-work (that is, the work of dialogue, of good interpersonal communication) or work of a business nature—all flows from the same source. It comes from the heart of the person, and as a Christian woman, I would say that within this heart, it comes from deeper still, from the heart of Christ drawing all of creation back to the dynamism of the Trinity. It is a flow, an energy, an attention, a presence, a being there, a focus, but as I use these words to describe work, you can see how these same words apply to prayer and to holy reading. These realities—prayer, reading, work—are all cosmic dimensions of a single force, a single unity.

What do I mean by this? Let me now focus specifically on Word and Work. Here, of course, I speak as a christian nun, living in a monastery. I cannot speak as anyone else, and yet, because I believe that we are all in this together, because I see that as a human person, what is genuine for me is probably also true for you potentially, even if not fully actually, I believe I speak for all of us. I am here, not as an expert or as a teacher, but as a fellow traveler with you. Perhaps on our life journeys some of us have gone through different doorways or have had various experiences. Our wounds and our blessings may vary, but we are all on the same journey together and I believe we shall find we have much more in common than we think. We might use different terminology or jargon, but often our basic core experiences are the same.

By the Word, I am referring to Christ. Yet in the context of this lecture, I mean holy reading, *lectio divina*, on the Scriptures, the Word of God. Holy reading and meditation on the Scriptures has been a tradition in all the great religions. The Hindus have the vedas, their holy scriptures. (As an aside, it is interesting to note that in the twelfth century, when the Cistercians were writing their many commentaries on the Song of Songs, the Hindus were also writing the Gita Govinda, a commentary very similar to those on the Song of Songs.) In Buddhism, in the Theravadan School, there has been a special emphasis on the reading and meditation of scriptures, but the Mahayana School and the Zen Buddhists also have their own tradition on this order. We all know the special place that meditation on the Koran holds for the Muslim, and certainly we are even more familiar with all the rabbinical commentaries which came from a tradition of meditation and then interpretation and commentary on the Word of God.

In the christian monastic tradition, this prayerful meditation, this holy reading of the Scriptures, has been practised by the earliest desert fathers living the eremitical (hermit) life, and the cenobitic monks and nuns living in communities down the ages into our own time. The classic 'back-bone' to this method of prayerful reading was provided by a twelfth-century carthusian monk, Guigo II. He divided *lectio* into four phases: reading, meditation, prayer, and contemplation. One of the most recent and best books explaining this tradition was written by a benedictine sister, Macrina Wiederkehr in 1988. It is called *A Tree Full of Angels: Seeing the Holy in the Ordinary*.[1]

Only five years earlier, Basil Pennington also treated this in his book, *Monastery: Prayer, Work, Community*.

In our christian tradition, Jesus himself first taught us *lectio*. In the resurrection account of the Gospel of Luke, two disciples on the road to Emmaus, not knowing the stranger walking with them on the road, are helped to gradually meet Jesus in the scriptures before they are ready to see that he is there in their midst. Luke writes:

> Then Jesus quoted them passage after passage from the writings of the prophets, beginning with the book of Gen-

1. Macrina Wiederkehr, *A Tree Full of Angels* (San Francisco: Harper and Row, 1988).

esis and going right on through the Scriptures, explaining
what the passages meant and what they said about himself.
(Lk 34:13–53)

First the apostles read and reflect on the Word of God and
then come to a real meeting with the person of Jesus. This is
what holy reading is all about: a reading and reflection which
leads to a meeting with the presence of the Risen Christ.

In the Book of Acts,[2] Luke tells us that the treasurer of
Ethiopia was traveling through the Gaza desert returning from
Jerusalem after worshiping in the temple. An angel directed
Philip to meet this man on the road. The man was reading
aloud the Book of Isaiah. Philip, running along the side of his
chariot asked him: 'Do you understand what you are reading?'
The high-ranking treasurer answered: 'Of course not! How
can I understand when there is no one to instruct me?' So
he invited Philip into the chariot and before the day ended
he was baptized by Philip. Here again, the reading of Scripture
leads to an experience of God. This is holy reading. In earlier
centuries, many people did not know how to read, but they
had wonderful memories. When they heard something read to
them, they committed it to their memory and then reflected
on it periodically.

Many explanations of *lectio* have been given, but I will put it
as simply as possible. Open the Holy Scriptures. You might use
the Sunday Gospel, or perhaps a favorite passage you like, or
even a passage that puzzles you, that you cannot understand.
Read through that passage. It might be a paragraph; it might
be much shorter. If a word or particular line or phrase seems
to draw you, stay with it. Repeat it to yourself in your heart or
even out loud, if you wish. Slowly and quietly, you gain a new
understanding, or a fresh insight may come to you, or better
yet, a prayer may well up in your heart. Then, you may even

2. Ac 8:26–39.

pass to a deeper level where you are so drawn by this word or passage that you have to stay with it. You may even experience the presence of Jesus. Perhaps you cannot put a name to this Presence, but you do know that you are in a holy Presence. As Jacob said: 'This is a holy place.'[3] And even beyond this level of sensitivity, you may completely lose your sense of yourself and simply become engrossed in an awareness so powerful and so subtle that your I-consciousness drops away. This is what I mean by contemplation, which is the deepest level of this holy reading. Everyone comes to this experience from a different place and each period of *lectio* is different. Just as an encounter with a real friend is different each time it happens, so it is with *lectio*. One person I know experiences *lectio* in such a way that she feels she is becoming exposed to the sun. She feels very vulnerable, very fragile.

Some people change the pronouns in a passage. For example, in the Gospel of Mark, in the passage where Jesus meets the rich young man,[4] we read that Jesus looked at him with love. I might take just that one line and change it to: 'Jesus, you look at me with love. Jesus, you look at me with love,' repeating that passage over and over again. Perhaps I feel drawn to stay with that line for ten minutes or even a half hour. Or perhaps, after a short while, I feel it is time to move on to another line or two. I read some more, maybe even the entire paragraph. I may find another line that draws me. I may not. Perhaps, after reading for some time, or after trying to pray through a passage, nothing seems to attract me or I feel distracted with other concerns. What then? If this happens day after day, it may be that I am taking the wrong time of the day for prayer. Maybe I should take the morning instead of the evening or vice versa. Each person has to discover his or her own 'prime time' and

3. Gen 28:17.
4. Mk 10:17–21.

prayer requires prime time. Perhaps you are exhausted and need to sleep for three days before you can even begin to think of sitting quietly with anything. But you may also discover that you begin this reading full of care and concerns, and gradually, those concerns drop away and you find yourself becoming very still and quiet. This kind of experience is a gift. Always be grateful for it. Thank God in your heart when this happens.

There is something else which may happen with *lectio*. You may end the period feeling very dry. You got nothing from it; it was even a waste of time. Then, later in the day, the meaning of a passage or line opens up for you at the least expected time—in the middle of the supermarket or while you are driving somewhere. Or perhaps you are really grappling with a situation in your life, with a person, or with a decision to be made, and suddenly, the word in the Scriptures that you had thought was completely closed to you, opens up and gives you an unbelievable solution, a real word of wisdom for your life. The more time you give to *lectio*, the more this sort of thing can happen. And yet, it is always gift. We cannot demand that it happen. We cannot produce it. We cannot force it. We cannot program it. It is a gentle process and we are not in control.

I'd like to mention one other kind of experience people sometimes have. Occasionally, something in the Scriptures jars you. Perhaps you really disagree with it. Or you read something about Jesus and ask: 'Why did he do that? Why was he so cruel to that woman?' You find yourself becoming very angry. Stay with your anger. Something important is happening. Using Jungian terminology, I would say you are meeting something in your shadow. Some important emotions are surfacing, perhaps some important repressed material is surfacing. Let it happen but do not force it. Always be led. You are not in control. Yet some very important, even some extraordinary healing can take place. One time this past year I was walking in our fields reading some Scripture, and when I came to a certain line, out of the clear blue, I burst into tears. A flood of emotions surfaced but also a deep revelation about myself and eventually a solution to a difficulty I was having. This sort of thing does not happen everyday. I do not expect *lectio* to be an adjunct therapy, and yet, healing often does come because the Word is present and active, like a two-edged sword. At other times this Word can be so gentle, so calming to my spirit. I can never predict. It is a holy adventure. You have to be open to surprises! You learn to bend and flex, to be supple and allow God to take the initiative, to melt into his presence.

As you can see, holy reading naturally becomes more than a reading of Scriptures. It becomes a reading of life, a reading of my responses to life, of my feelings and emotions, of my inter-personal relationships. If holy reading is completely divorced form the rest of my day and activity, something is wrong. I need some help with it. *Lectio* flows into life and life flows into *lectio*. Word and Work.

When I say 'work', some people may react with annoyance: 'I came here to hear about contemplation, not about work. I want to leave my job back at the office.' Other people may be getting bored with all this theory and would like to get back to work. They can see everything piling up and waiting for them when they get home. But work is integral to everything we are talking about! Prayer, contemplation, holy reading lead naturally to *praxis*, not only the *praxis* of repeating a prayer-word or a line of Scripture, but the practice of finding God, of being centered in all our daily life and activity. And often that activity is our work.

In the monastic tradition, especially among cenobites (those living in communities) work has always been very important and many stories and anecdotes demonstrate this. Keeping the hands busy was, and still is, a way that helps many monks and nuns still their minds. Work keeps the body physically sound and the mind in touch with reality. When someone knocks at our door and wants to enter our community, I find out a great deal about her just by watching her work. It shows me how she interacts with others, how she accepts responsibility, how she lets go of her own methods of doing things, and how she takes initiative when a situation calls for that.

The monastic tradition has provided a kind of school to teach us how to work and to handle what happens to us as we work. A favorite story comes from Pachomius, one of the very early monks.

> Remembering the promise he had made to God, Pachomius began with his brother to build a larger monastery, to receive those who would come to this life. As they were building, Pachomius was extending the place with this aim in view, while his brother, John, wanting more withdrawal apart, was making it smaller. [I think we have a power struggle here!] While they were building the monastery's wall, they had a slight disagreement with each other. His brother angrily retorted, 'Stop being so conceited!' Hearing this word, Pachomius' heart was agitated. When he saw that his heart was embittered at this little word, he was deeply distressed and said, 'I am not yet faithful, and I am still far from God whose will I promised to follow.[5]

The manuscript then describes how Pachomius went to a little underground place in the village and spent the night in prayer. You can see him struggling with his emotions, trying to come to grips with what is going on in his heart, to read his feelings and then bring them to the Lord for healing. It was a hot summer night and the brick he was standing on soon disintegrated. Then the manuscript says: 'At daybreak he stopped praying and went again with his brother to work at their building'.

A few days later his brother hurled another remark at him. When he heard it, Pachomius' heart was embittered and

---

5. There are various manuscript traditions for the Life of Pachomius and I am taking this story from two manuscripts: the First Greek Life and then the First Sahidic life which have been translated by Cistercian Publications.

seeing the agitation of his heart he did as he had done the first time. He spent the whole night in prayer so that the brick on which he stood turned to mud under his feet. From that day on, these types of thoughts no longer made him angry, because God granted the request he had made to him. Pachomius also eagerly asked the Lord to enable him to accomplish the other commandments that are written in the holy Scriptures. After that his brother died.[6]

While we may object to this passage and say: 'Feelings are good. There is no way he could have learned to work with them after only two tries'. We have to learn how to read a passage like this, and to realize that the story is trying to tell us something. First of all, there is the importance of the two brothers working together because this is the way interpersonal conflicts surface. Then we see Pachomius spending the whole night in prayer, asking God to change his heart. Note that he does not ask God to convert his brother! He is asking God to change his own heart. He realized therefore, that the emotions and the problem are inside him, not outside. And after the whole night in prayer, he finds himself the very next day back at square one. So he has to return and work with himself, asking God again for healing. God hears his prayer and then, the manuscript says, his brother died! You almost get the feeling here that his brother's presence was precisely the agent God used, or the circumstance, for Pachomius' self-knowledge, and when the lesson is learned, the situation changes.

I think that work situations in the monastic life (and no doubt in your life, too) often reveal this sort of dynamic. Perhaps with this one difference: you can go home at 6 p.m. and forget the fellow who always presses the wrong button in you, while in a monastery, you have to live with the people with whom you

6. Armand Veilleux, trans., *Pachomian Koinonia*, 3 Vols. (Kalamazoo: Cistercian Publications, 1980) I (CS45): pp. 307–308, 429–430.

work, and an interpersonal conflict really has to be resolved. It is challenging to live in that environment but I believe it is also very healthy.

One other thing I have noticed about work in a monastery: it is not always done in the most efficient way. I cannot make that a global statement because there are in our monasteries many very efficiently run industries that would be models for any small business. But there are always times when a monk or nun runs across a situation which seems uselessly inefficient. Yet the job always gets done, and the lesson I have been learning in these situations is simply to let go. My ego is very keen on problem-solving for others. Gradually I am learning my own co-dependency patterns. The world can live without me and the monastery could really go on quite well if I dropped dead. Sometimes those are hard lessons! Another principle here is to do the work simply to be doing it.

In a monastery, at least in ours, jobs can frequently be changed. We cannot develop a comfortable niche where we feel secure. Most of all, we cannot begin to identify too much with a role, with a *persona*. We really have to let go of that and find an identity within ourself. This is what new people usually find the most difficult in our monasteries. They enter after having held professional positions and they have often found their identity in their role. Suddenly all that is stripped away and they find themselves peeling potatoes and not doing it very well. That's hard on the ego. It can be great fun for the first week and something to write home about, but after three years, it gets scary. One of our american abbots tells of having been in the monastery some ten years when all his friends were getting responsible positions or were being sent off to study in Rome. One day the abbot called him into his office and asked if he were ready to take on more responsibility. He had been waiting for that question. When he happily said he was, the abbot asked if he would take charge of the shoe-shining equipment kept in a single black box. We can laugh at that or we can say: 'How stupid, how silly!' It does make a great story, but there is more to it. This monk—now a very capable abbot running a large abbey—had to learn that his personal identity was a gift from God and did not depend on his role, his job, or his career. His goodness and capability were within and could not be lost. Psychologists tell us today that this sort of wisdom is the task of people in mid-life, but monastics have known this truth for a long time and they have found ways of developing it in people without even giving it names.

Here again, Word and Work interact. Work which is repetitious and devoid of challenge can have a negative influence on a person's life unless something else is going on inside, unless the Word is addressing this person, unless it includes an invitation, a question, and the possibility of response.

Responding to the Word of God through my work and the care I exercise in doing it has particular emphasis in the Rule of Benedict. The thirty-first chapter of the Rule is dedicated to the cellarer, the manager, one of the busiest people in a monastery . Nevertheless, if a cellarer is really living the Rule of Benedict, you will not feel this person is scattered or does not have time to stop for a moment. Here are some of the things Benedict has to say about the cellarer:

> He may not hurt the feelings of the brethren. Should a brother perchance ask for something that is unreasonable, let him not grieve his confrere by belittling him, but reasonably and humbly disallow the improper request.[7]
>
> He shall be most loving in his care for the sick, the children, the guests, and the poor, because he doubtless knows that he will have to give an account of all these things on the day of judgement.[8]

7. Basilius Steidle, trans., *The Rule of St. Benedict* (Canon City: Holy Cross Abbey, 1967) Chapter 31.6, 7.

8. *Ibid.* 31:9.

He shall regard the utensils of the monastery and all its property as if they were the vessels of the altar. Let him not think that he may neglect anything.[9]

He shall not be a prodigal or a wastrel of the substance of the cloister, but he shall manage everything in moderation . . . [10]

He must above all things have humility, and if he has nothing to give, let him give in answer a good word, as it is written: 'A good word exceeds the best gift'.[11]

If the community be rather large, let him be given help so that with their assistance he may with a calm mind discharge the office entrusted to him. The articles that are to be asked for and the things that are to be given out shall be asked for and distributed at convenient hours, so that no one need be troubled or grieved in the house of God.[12]

We have here an excellent management guide, one written in the sixth century during a period of barbarian invasions and great social upheaval. Yet, in it are norms that reflect peace and good judgement, discretion and wholeness, balance and care.

In our present time many of us are becoming aware of the importance of centering, of giving ourselves wholly to a task with an undivided heart, of acting in peace without concentrating on the result.

These attitudes need not be the prerogative of monks and nuns. They belong to any person who desires to live a holistic life. But just as Word and Work interact, I also believe that the gift of our times will be an on-going dialogue between monastics and persons living in the marketplace. In this way, I believe, the contemplative tradition will become more visible in the West. We owe this gift of mutuality to one another so

9. *Ibid.* 31:10, 11.
10. *Ibid.* 31:12.
11. *Ibid.* 31:13, 14.
12. *Ibid.* 31:17, 18, 19.

that the Word and Work of peace will reign in our hearts and in our universe.

During this period of work, one thing you may have realized is that talk and chatter is not necessarily an outside, spoken activity. When we become quiet, or attempt to be quiet, a million thoughts invade our mind and heart and the chatter simply moves inward: 'Why are we doing this anyway? This is really dumb. I wonder how I can move this root out of here? I wish I had a better tool. Gee, this is so peaceful. I wish I could stay out here another hour.' This internal self-talk is sometimes nourishing and sometimes distracting. Here it's time to talk about listening . . . or perhaps to listen about listening. The Rule of Benedict begins: 'Listen, my son [and daughter] to the precepts of your master and incline the ear of your heart.' This is a very powerful image: 'Incline the ear of your heart.' When you incline your bodily posture, you indicate an interest in something. And if you incline the ear of your heart, this implies that your heart is listening. You listen with your heart—not with your head in a rational way which sizes up the situation and makes a judgement—but with your heart. You are simply present to the reality, not judging it or coming to a rational conclusion, but rather 'being with' the other or the other situation. What is this person or this text of scripture saying to me? What is this situation requiring of me? Some years ago Victor Frankl was my teacher. He used to explain to us that a situation in life asks you a question and there is really only one right answer for you—as a person—to give. As you discover this answer, you also find meaning. Often when we lose meaning in life it's because we have stopped listening to our hearts or to the requirements of life around us.

This attitude of listening is essential for *lectio*. Yet as we listen to the Word of God, we may feel some anguish or some poverty and vulnerability. We may realize that we don't 'have our act together.' This is good!! This means that God is active and we are listening. We do not have a lollipop God or a dispensing machine God who keeps things nice and cozy for us. Rather, God asks a question of us, not as a tyrant, to trip us up, but as a challenger, to help us grow. Victor Frankl also used to say that when we truly love a person, we see his or her potential, even, perhaps, when neither the other person nor other people see it. The one who truly loves can see this potential. This is much more true of God, who sees our true potential and who loves us into Being, who may at times stretch us to help us grow into the Self we are called to be, the transcendent self, living beyond the ego, continuing the process of creation all around us. Listening to the Word, listening to reality brings us to this true life, this abundant life we hear about in the Gospels.

Sometimes as we begin to listen, we are overwhelmed by our sinfulness, our selfishness. This should not lead to discouragement. Instead, it is a wonderful discovery because it leads us out of ourselves in love to our neighbor.

In all of this, patience is the key. Learning to do *lectio* takes time. It is not an overnight process. It is a life work. The more you do it, the more you 'catch on'. *Lectio* implies a willingness to be transformed. Something happens to us in *lectio*. When you sit in the sun, you may feel you've done nothing at all, but then discover your face has tanned. Something has happened to you without your realizing it. The sun touches us on the outside; *lectio* touches us inside. It is like letting the sun shine in your heart. You may feel burned at times, but usually, you know something has warmed you and changed you in a positive way. Something beautiful gradually takes shape. In a few weeks, a few months, a few years, you discover you are no longer the person you were before. Real growth has taken place.

Lectio should be part of the balance and rhythm in our life. One of the twelfth-century Cistercian Fathers, Aelred of Rievaulx, wrote in one of his homilies:

Let us prepare a spiritual home that our Lord may come to us. If our soul has become the home we have described, it is necessary that two women live in it: one to sit at Jesus' feet that she may hear his words, the other to wait on him that he may eat. If Mary alone is in that house, there will be no one to feed the Lord. Therefore, Martha signifies that action by which we labor for Christ. Mary, however, signifies that rest by which a person delights in the sweetness of God through reading, prayer, and contemplation. As long as Christ is poor and walks on the earth, hungry, thirsty and tempted, both these women must live in one house—that is, both these actions must be performed in the same soul.[13]

When Saint Anthony of the desert, considered the Father of Monks, was seeking to know what God wanted of him, he had a vision, perhaps a dream, in which he was plaiting reeds. Then, after a while, he saw himself getting up to pray. Later he returned to the reeds; then he saw himself getting up to pray. Later he returned to the reeds, and then later again to prayer. And so he learned the important rule of alternation . . . not choosing one activity over another, but combining both in a healthy rhythm. In the fourteenth century, a flemish mystic, Jan Van Ruusbroeck, would write:

Perfection is not a matter of choosing between these obligations—of accepting one and rejecting another. On the contrary, we must harmonize the two, achieve a perfect balance between them.[14]

Aelred of Rievaulx also wrote of the alternation between work and rest in *The Mirror of Charity*. Building on the Genesis creation account, in which God works six days and then celebrates a sabbath, Aelred speaks of the six days of work as

13. Aelred of Rievaulx, *Sermo in Assumptione* 19.5; *Aelredi Rievallensis Sermones I-XLVI*, ed. Gaetano Raciti, CCCM 2a (Turnholt: Brepols, 1989) 148. I am indebted to Dr Marsha Dutton for calling this passage to my attention.

14. I am embarrassed to admit that I have lost my reference to this lovely passage.

the time of acquiring virtue. The first day is faith, the second, hope, and so on through temperance, prudence, judgement, fortitude, and justice. The seventh and sabbath day is Charity. You can love both the good and the bad, Aelred explained. To love what is evil leads to self-centeredness; to love what is good leads to Charity.

Before you decide that I've gone off on a tangent, let me explain that here again we are dealing with rhythm and balance but the rhythm and balance are within and become intermingled or interchanged. Work can become restful and full of peace (even in the busiest circumstances) and rest itself has an element of work in it, especially when the rest is Charity.

Gandhi used to say that he never needed a vacation because he found a way to rest within his activity. He found a stillpoint in the center of all that he did. Similarly, Jung claimed that the secret to mental health was not in doing what you like, but in learning to like what you do. There is a lot of truth in this.

How do we come to this kind of holistic living, this living in the center, in the heart, in Christ? Isaac of Stella, another twelfth-century Cistercian wrote: 'Wisdom is learnt when at leisure, but not by the lazy. No leisure is more busy, no free time more full of toil than when wisdom is being earned, when the Word of God is being consulted.'

And so we find ourselves back at *lectio*—consulting the Word of God. How do we really learn this process of listening, of consulting the Word? Some learn it gradually and seem to fall into it by intuition, as if following a path which leads gradually ever deeper into the forest, this forest being within the heart. Others of us have to be jolted into it. My own time (not that I have by any means arrived) came a number of years ago when I learned I had multiple sclerosis. At first, I was not allowed to drive on expressways because my type of MS sometimes causes seizures. I remember how, during those early years, I resented having to drive in the slow lane. It became a symbol of my whole life: everything had moved to the slow lane. But

I had always enjoyed the fast lane. The faster the better. The more I could do (all at one time), the more fulfilled I felt. Now suddenly I had to take rest periods during the day, and do things slowly. But I discovered something altogether new. The route I drove each day took me into a beautiful park. I had never noticed the park before. Each day as I drove through the park, I came to love it more and more. Suddenly I began to wonder why I had ever wanted to drive on expressways. This one symbol began to spill over in so many areas of life, and it remains even though now the seizures are controlled and I can take the car back into the fast lane if I choose. I would suggest that you sometime try to move into the slow lane for a few hours, even for a day. If it takes you ten minutes to walk to the library, try to do it in twenty. If you usually eat a meal in thirty minutes, try forty-five. Better yet, go off to some cabin for twenty-four hours and leave your watch at home. You will know when it's time to leave. We seldom realize how hooked we can be into time slots and knowing what time it is. Some of us almost panic when we do not know what time it is.

There are many experiments along this line. The idea is, as it were, to stand on your head and look at reality upside down or inside out until work becomes prayer and prayer becomes work, a work that refreshes us. When you become bored at work, try paying minute attention to everything you are doing. Boredom will immediately disappear. Only lack of attention causes boredom.

All this translates directly back into the level of self-tran-scendent love or charity. When we pay full attention to the other—whether it be our neighbor, our work, or the person of God, of Christ—; when we work with a listening heart—not for particular gain, but simply to be in the presence of that other—, then we are in a center where Love dwells and opposites meet. As the psalmist says: 'Peace and justice will embrace'. Then, instead of the danger of manipulating reality or the other person, there is a sense of wonder and gratitude, awe and marvel. On the Mount of Transfiguration, the apostles said: 'Truly it is good to be here. Let us build three tents.' On the road to Emmaus, the apostles begged Jesus to stay longer with them. This kind of experience is open to everyone of us. It is not reserved for mystics or monks. It touches the mystic and monk inside each of our hearts.

Thomas Merton once eloquently, in a passage whose source I failed to note down but with which I agree completely, called *lectio divina* 'the one transcendent activity of the contemplative life [which] . . . embraces all other activities and elevates them to its own supreme level of liberty and rest.'

RECOMMENDATIONS FOR FURTHER READING

Charles Cummings, ocso, *Monastic Practices*. Kalamazoo: Cistercian Publications. 1986.

Esther De Waal, *Living with Contradiction. Reflections on the Rule of St Benedict*. New York: Harper. 1989.

—————. *Seeking God. The Way of St Benedict*. London: Collins-Collegeville: Liturgical Press. 1984.

Thomas Spidlek, ed., *Drinking from the Hidden Fountain. A Patristic Breviary*. London: New City Press. 1992. Kalamazoo: Cistercian Publications. 1994.

Norvene Vest, *No Moment Too Small*. Kalamazoo: Cistercian Publications - Cambridge: Cowley Publications. 1994.

Adalbert de Vogüé, *Reading Saint Benedict. Reflections on the Rule*. Kalamazoo: Cistercian Publications. 1994.

BEING AWAKE:

Reflections on the Workshop

Jasper Green Pennington

In Huston Smith's *The World Religions*,[1] Buddha (Siddahartha Gautama Sakyas) is asked 'Are you a god?' 'No.' 'An angel?' 'No.' 'A saint?' 'No.' 'Then what are you?' And Buddha answered, 'I am awake'.

Being awake to life in all its dimensions is the human quest, the human journey. It can be described in any number of ways including the longing for success or happiness or wisdom or whatever. And it can be described as the longing for God which so undergirds most of the religious traditions of the world, including Christianity.

The 'restless heart' of Augustine, reluctant humanity being pursued by the 'hound of heaven' of Francis Thompson, the voices of the Old Testament Prophets, the invitations of Jesus to those who would follow God, the activities of a Mother Teresa and the contemplative life of a Thomas Merton are all strands of the call to 'be awake', to 'be attentive' to the 'pearls of great price', the 'lost coins' of life. Which is object and which is subject is often a moot point in this process of living in and with God.

1. Harper, 1991, p. 82.

Drawing on the anglican, lutheran, orthodox and roman catholic spiritual traditions, some fifty participants spent a week together in August 1991[2] in a workshop entitled 'The Contemplative Path: Rediscovering a Lost Tradition.' Made possible by a generous grant from the Fetzer Institute of Kalamazoo, Michigan and organized and sponsored by the Institute of Cistercian Studies at Western Michigan University with the collaboration of the Fellowship of Saint Alban and Saint Sergius (USA), the Workshop was moderated by the Reverend M. Basil Pennington, OCSO. Participants were treated to lectures by scholars and monastics representing the four traditions, and had opportunities to experience various types of prayer and meditation techniques as well as yoga. And each day was framed by the Daily Offices as used in one of the four traditions.

The Reverend Professor Paul Bradshaw of the University of Notre Dame discussed the Divine Office, distinguishing its Monastic and Cathedral styles of prayer. The Very Reverend Father Michael St. Andrew discussed the 'Shape of the Orthodox Liturgy' and led a choir practice. The Reverend Professor John Breck of Saint Vladimir's Orthodox Seminary talked of the 'Jesus Prayer' and its use in the Orthodox Tradition. The Reverend William Forrest, OSB, of Saint Gregory's Abbey, Three Rivers, Michigan, spoke of the benedictine life in the Anglican Tradition. Some fascinating (and challenging) workshop sessions were led by Lady Mary Stewart of London, England, on 'Incorporating the Body into Prayer' with some yoga exercises which quickly separated the 'fit' from the 'unfit'!

The Reverend Dr Gustav Kopka spoke on 'Piety and Pietism in the Protestant Tradition', drawing on writings of Martin Luther, Johann Arndt, Jakob Boehme, and Paul Gerhardt and

2. August 4–10.

the great legacy of German hymnody. The Reverend Roufail S. Michail of Saint Mark's Coptic Orthodox Church, Troy, Michigan, discussed the Desert Spirituality of the Copts and led us in the evening office. Father Basil discussed the creation of a contemplative life-style in contemporary society and all participated in experiences of 'centering prayer'. Sister GilChrist Lavigne, OCSO, of Our Lady of the Mississippi Abbey in Dubuque, Iowa, brought a delightful scholarship to a presentation of 'Word and Work', noting the benedictine motto, *Ora et labora*. And the Reverend Richard Herbel, OSB, Lutheran monk of Saint Augustine's House in Oxford, Michigan, shared something of the long story of monasticism and the longing for God in the Lutheran Tradition. Our hosts, Mr Robert F. Lehman, President of the Fetzer Institute, and Dr E. Rozanne Elder, Director of the Cistercian Institute, and their staffs, provided splendid hospitality for us and stimulating resources for further thought and study.

Rediscovering a Lost Tradition seemed a misnomer in the very rich atmosphere of the Workshop. 'Remembering Some Forgotten Traditions' might have been a more apt title as the participants shared the experiences of their various cultural, spiritual, personal, and corporate responses to the 'longing for God' which is so much a stimulus to the human journey.

That the 'longing for God' is expressed in many voices was clear in the presentations by scholars and monastics. Being 'awake' to God in the religious and cultural traditions in which humans find themselves is clearly an ongoing task . . . and one which needs to be refocused again and again.

The four basic spiritual types, drawn on and expanded by Carl Gustav Jung and others (reflective, emotional, active, experimental) underlie the prayer traditions and styles among Anglicans, Lutherans, Orthodox, and Roman Catholics—traditions which are given recognition in both public and private prayer and in the balance between work and worship, active and passive use of the imagination, the outer and inner life.

Most of us who work or live in parishes find that keeping a balance between an activity-oriented social life and the reflective and thoughtful time needed to give purpose and meaning to it all is a frustrating challenge. Remembering our roots, recovering our traditions of prayer and conversation with God and being intentional about the use of 'memory, reason, and skill'[3] are foundation stones which have to be returned to again and again. Sorting out the responses we want to make to God who is ever present in the midst of the daily crises of life and the 'things which take just a minute' is a critical task of the Church and its leadership in today's world.

Drawing on the rich thought of the spiritual fathers and mothers of the past, each tradition presented insights as stimulating and strengthening for us as they must have been for earlier God-seekers. Theophan the Recluse[4], quoted by Father Breck as saying that 'true prayer is to stand with the mind in the heart before God, and to go on standing before Him ceaselessly, day and night, until the end of life', expresses recognition of the presence of God who teaches us to pray and to go on praying in lives which are occupied by the 'secular' as well as the 'sacred'. Echoes of 'standing' before God, or sitting, or sleeping, or working, or in our distractions, well out of the words of the gospel hymn by C. Austin Miles:[5] 'He walks with me and He talks with me, and He tells me I am His own . . . .' This profound understanding that God binds and braids and integrates all of our life into a pattern and image of his making gives a kind of joy and expectation and excitement to the times when we can withdraw and be still in a more intentional way.

Dr Kopka, in discussing german Pietism, spoke of *pietas* as having to do with a loving loyalty, with a certain stance of

---

3. *The Book of Common Prayer*, Eucharistic Prayer C, p. 370.
4. *The Art of Prayer*, pp. 63 & 190.
5. *The New Church Hymnal* (Lexicon Music Inc., 1976), p. 241.

the thoughts, actions and relationships towards the state. It is this stance towards God which offers some new insights to our generation of manically busy people who yet yearn for god. Every place can become a *templum*, a 'holy place'[6] where one can 'take time to be holy' and 'speak oft with the Lord'.[7] The search for interiority among Protestants seems naturally to be reflected in hymnody. Quoting poet and pastor Paul Gerhardt (1606–1676), Dr Kopka called our attention to *The Lutheran Book of Worship*, which includes ten out of some one hundred thirty-four German and fourteen Latin hymns. Their importance in eighteenth-century english piety is attested to by John Wesley's translations, including

> Jesus, thy boundless love to me,
> No thought can reach, no tongue declare;
> Unite my thankful heart to thee,
> And reign without a rival there!
> Thine wholly, thine alone, I am;
> Be thou alone my constant flame.[8]

and Catherine Winkworth's (1829–1878) translation of Martin Schalling's (1532–1608) hymn

> Lord, thee I love with all my heart;
> I pray thee, ne'r from me depart;
> With tender mercy cheer me.[9]

It seemed only too obvious during the Workshop that the traditions of christian spirituality have not been lost but rather overwhelmed by the press of an active and thoughtless society where immediate solutions to the great issues of life have become so noisy as to be 'clanging gongs' which threaten to

6. Kopka, p. 2.
7. William D. Longstaff. 'Take Time to Be Holy', in *The New Church Hymnal* (Lexicon, 1976) p. 155.
8. *Lutheran Book of Worship* (Lutheran Church in America, 1978) p. 336.
9. *Ibid*, p. 325.

drown out the 'still small voice of God'. I found Professor Bradshaw's statement, that 'what matters is that the Church should
pray, not that every individual should participate in it', to be
a helpful and broadening concept. Certainly one of the issues
constantly being dealt with is the issue of guilt from parishioners
not able to attend public worship as faithfully as they feel they
ought. With this comes the subsequent loss of a sense of
spirituality in their lives, as if God could be found only in a
sacred building. It is disheartening. Being 'teachers of prayer'—
rather than administrators, social workers, building supervisors
and fund raisers—is part of the calling of the Christian, and especially of the ordained. This needs re-emphasizing in our day.

Expanding some of Professor Bradshaw's distinctions between 'cathedral' worship—led by ordained ministers, and
concerned with the externals of worship—and 'monastic'
prayer—an individual activity in which externals are dispensable or severely limited—one can see that for many people,
'monastic' prayer is in fact what they find most reachable, most
practical in their busy lives. Perhaps even seeing themselves
as 'monastics' having a 'rule of life' which undergirds their
secular employment and worldly responsibilities would help
them realize more fully that 'longing for God' which exists in
every human heart. Helping individuals to stretch and adjust
their experience of God so that they are not trapped and
discouraged by inherited prayer forms and habits could unleash
a whole new pleasure in God, a joy which is too often missing
as contemporary men and women struggle to reaffirm God
while coping with present realities.

During visits to Russia in 1984 and 1987, I was much impressed by the number of monastics who were living solitary
lives or living with only one or two others in order to continue a
kind of disciplined witness in the midst of religious oppression.
Keeping a 'rule of life' while employed in all kinds of 'secular'
work seems to exhibit the best of the christian call. Since
Vatican II, one sees something of this model among Western

religious who have found the larger monastery or convent unfulfilling. These adaptations to the changing needs of individuals and of the institutional Church in our century reaffirms the continuing call of God to 'a better country', to newness and freshness of life while still maintaining an awareness of community and service to it.

I found that the reminders about the prayer of the heart which Father Basil and Father John Breck brought us to complete a kind of circle in my life. So many people influence us as we grow. I recall how my Grandmother Pennington in her old age used to sit and read her Bible in a wonderfully peaceful and contemplative way. And I remember how she used to go to sleep with a prayer on her lips. I was impressed with that as a child, and long before I knew anything about the 'prayer of the heart' or 'the Jesus Prayer' or even Saint Paul's words, 'pray without ceasing', I was exposed to that way of life. And as I recall it, I am more than ever impressed with my grandmother because I doubt very much that she was familiar with much of the spiritual terminology which we discussed in this Workshop. However she 'longed for God' and responded out of the tradition of study and prayer which was common in her family and religious life.

Father Breck said that 'the deepest sadness and the greatest joy in christian life are caused by an innate longing for God, a passionate quest for intimate and eternal communion with the Persons of the Holy Trinity.'[10] Responding to this longing is not simple because it involves the wonderful complexities of our minds, bodies and spirits. The idea of loving God, that is the intellectual choice to look God-ward, is only the beginning. It becomes more complex as soon as we try to concentrate or even find a daily rhythm of waiting before God. And then we are challenged to do something with what we hear and we are

10. Above, p. 39.

immediately involved in further complexities. Yet the call to us is made again and again. Some wag told me recently in a Bible Study class that if Abraham had just stayed home we wouldn't be in this mess! Well, Abraham didn't stay home. He began a life of response, in spite of the very untidy and disconcerting realities of his life. And we must do the same.

Father Basil reminds us that we need to be as wise as serpents and as simple as doves in our contemplation and communion with God. Spiritual teachers have used various ascetical techniques to keep the dialogue simple. Because of our complexities and our creativities and our desires, keeping honest is not easy. And yet the longing for God is there. God keeps inviting us on the journey in spite of our inhibitions or lack of confidence or unworthiness or distractions. 'Resting in God' may not come easily. It may need to be preceded by a lot of discipline in just quieting down and allowing the inner and outer noises of our life to be washed away by the hand of God who reaches over the storms and winds for us.

In recent years I have found the need for complete silence to be a growing thing. The distractions of even the quiet noises of household equipment seem too loud. Even the music I love is a distraction and invasion. 'The hunger for stimuli that divert our attention from "the place of the heart" '[11] is an addiction of our society. The call to 'hesychast' prayer which 'signifies inner calm, stillness, silence'[12] can lead to tremendous blessings and reassurances which 'pass all understanding'. Being in a state of quiet attentiveness is to reach deep into the inner life and strength of God which is within each of us. 'Watch and pray' is the call of the forerunners of God in every generation and in most religious traditions East and West. Like Buddha, we are to 'be awake' to the touches of God in us and in the world around us.

11. Above, p. 41.
12. *Ibid.*

Seeing the 'prayer of the heart' and 'centering prayer' as inclusive of intercessory prayer and thanksgivings is, I think, an important concept. How often I have struggled to remember in prayer all the needs which I have been exposed to or have had brought to my attention during the day. Sometimes I have worried so about forgetting some request that my prayer time resembled nothing so much as a trip to the boss's office to bring him up-to-date on the affairs of the company! Being in God's presence, speaking the name of Jesus or some other personal word of love is to bring the complexities of the 'company' to God 'who is great and without limit' who 'upholds the whole universe'.[13] Psalm 139, *Domine, probasti*, gives us the right stance as we come into the presence of God: 'Lord, you have searched me out and known me; you know my sitting down and my rising up, you discern my thoughts from afar.[14] Our lives, which are both individual and corporate, are linked to the innermost needs and desires of the larger life and we braid the two together as we wait on God.

In the anglican tradition from which I come, we sometimes speak of ourselves as the 'both/and' people of God. This has something to do with the desire for balance between reason and emotion, intellect and heart, the english desire for 'decency and order', and awe before the mystery of God, the unexplainable. After centuries of religious strife, which continues only too obviously in our own day, the richness and variety of the several spiritual traditions represented in this Workshop offer us some wonderful new building blocks for the future. The prevalence and popularity of self-help books, the sales in Bibles and prayer books and reissues of spiritual classics, the writings of modern-day pilgrims and the rediscovered writings of holy men and women of the past—all these indicate that

13. Above, p. 51.
14. *The Book of Common Prayer*, p. 794.

the hunger for God has not been subsumed by materialism. *Lectio divina* is not only alive, but bringing a profit to publishers and booksellers throughout the western world.

Sister GilChrist writes that 'our wounds and our blessings may vary, but we are all on the same journey together'.[15] Living in a multi-cultural and multi-racial environment, as we do increasingly in North America, the Christian, if s/he is to be a person awake to the voices of those seeking God and to God speaking in many tongues, needs an alert response. Drawing on the contemplative paths of Christianity in its Anglican, Lutheran, Orthodox, Roman Catholic and yet other voices is to rediscover oneness in the midst of many. Like Pachomius, we must begin to 'build a larger monastery, to receive those who would come to this life'.[16] I believe it was Douglas Steere who wrote that prayer is a time to become human. In so many ways our spiritual traditions help us to become more fully human and awake to our humanity, and thus to the humanity of others. Again, like Pachomius, we ask God to change our hearts, to enlighten our minds, to development our self-knowledge, including the knowledge of our spiritual ancestries as illustrated to some extent by this Workshop on the contemplative path.

The historian Arnold Toynbee observed that 'There is no one alive today who knows enough to say with confidence whether one religion has been greater than all others'.[17] The re-examination of personality types of Jung and others and their broad application in many aspects of life, including the spiritual, give us some wider elbow-room in the examination of the life of prayer and in an unbiased look at not only the various and sometimes separate traditions of Christianity, but also the whole ecumenical and inter-faith dialogue. All of us

15. Above, p. 94.
16. Cited above, p. 100.
17. Cited by Smith, p. 6.

incorporate many 'types' within ourselves and our spiritual, cultural, economic and political traditions. Some years ago Avery Dulles in *Models of the Church*[18] presented a variety of early ecclesiastical and biblical models of church government and organization as a way of loosening up our inherited concepts. Today with the re-examination of the role of women in Church and society, in human sexuality, in the rebuilding of legal and economic and political structures in various parts of the world, we are more than ever aware that the human spirit has been shackled rather than freed by oppressive human history. Freeing our institutions and re-examining our inherited religious and cultural traditions may make it possible for God to be heard in new ways and to speak across history and culture and religious traditions and encourage many more to seek the Way.

A challenge for all religious is to be awake to the essentials so that the longing for God comes through the accumulations of the past and the present cultures and religious traditions. Saint Basil says that 'the human person is an animal who received the command to become God, that is, to become a participant in the very life of God through the deifying energies or operations of the indwelling Spirit'.[19] Remembering the forgotten traditions of prayer and the ways to God was richly shared by the Anglican, Lutheran, Orthodox and Roman Catholic scholars, monastics and participants in the August 1991 Workshop. It was a pleasure to find much of it taking place in the beautiful setting of the Fetzer Institute which is itself devoted to the wider integration of the minds, bodies and spirits through which God touches us.

18. Dublin: Gill and Macmillan, 1976, 1978, 1988.
19. Cited above, p. 40.

CONTRIBUTORS

Paul F. Bradshaw is Professor Liturgy at the University of Notre Dame. Born and educated in England, he holds an undergraduate degree from the University of Cambridge and doctorates from both London and Oxford. His studies of *Ordination Rites* and *Daily Prayer in the Early Church* have established him as a leading liturgical scholar on both sides of the Atlantic. A priest of the Church of England, he has recently published *Two Ways of Praying. An Introduction to Liturgical Prayer.*

John Breck, a priest of the Orthodox Church in America, holds degrees from Brown University, Yale Divinity School and the University of Heidelberg. The author of *The Power of the Word*, on Scripture in Orthodox interpration, he is professor of New Testament and Ethics at Saint Vladimir's Seminary, Crestwood, New York, and editor of *Saint Vladimir's Theological Quarterly.*

E. Rozanne Elder is Editorial Director of Cistercian Publications and Director of the Institute of Cistercian Studies at Western Michigan University.

Gustav Kopka, Jr. is pastor of St Peter's Lutheran Church in Warren, Michigan. A native of Germany, he studied both Theology and Classics, in which he holds a doctorate from the University of Texas-Austin, after coming to the United States. Before accepting the position of Director of the Michigan

Ecumenical Forum and then moving into parish ministry, he served in campus ministries in Texas, North Dakota, and Michigan.

GilChrist Lavigne, OCSO, is a cistercian nun of Our Lady of the Mississippi Abbey, Dubuque, Iowa. Born in Montreal and bilingual in French and English, she first entered monastic life with the Benedictines of Perpetual Adoration. At the present time she serves on the Board for East-West Monastic Dialogue, and has worked in her community as a teacher, a computer programmer and a candy maker.

Robert F. Lehman trained in both law and theology. He is President and CEO of the Fetzer Institute, Kalamazoo, and Chairman of the Board of Trustees of the Fetzer Memorial Trust. Before joining Fetzer, he worked successively as Assistant Dean for Academic Affairs at the School of Law of Indiana University and Vice President and Director of International Programs at the Kettering Foundation.

M. Basil Pennington, OCSO, a monk of Saint Joseph's Abbey, Spencer, Massachusetts, has spent several years on assignment at Our Lady of Joy Abbey, Lantao (Hong Kong). A noted author of books on the spiritual life, he holds degrees in theology and canon law from the Gregorian University, Rome. A member of the Board of Directors and the founding editor of Cistercian Publications, he is also well known for the Centering Prayer Workshops he conducts in the United States and abroad.

Jasper Green Pennington is rector of Saint Luke's Episcopal Church, Ypsilanti, Michigan, and historiographer of the Diocese of Michigan. He holds degrees in music, history, librarianship, and theology from Western Michigan University, the University of the South at Sewanee, and Notre Dame. Before taking his present pastoral position, he worked as the founding librarian at the Archbishop Fulton J. Sheen Library and Archives in Rochester, New York.

CISTERCIAN PUBLICATIONS, INC.
TITLES LISTING

—CISTERCIAN TEXTS—

THE WORKS OF BERNARD OF CLAIRVAUX

Apologia to Abbot William
Five Books on Consideration: Advice to a Pope
Homilies in Praise of the Blessed Virgin Mary
The Life and Death of Saint Malachy the Irishman
Love without Measure. Extracts from the Writings
of St Bernard (Paul Dimier)
On Grace and Free Choice
On Loving God (Emero Stiegman)
The Parables of Saint Bernard (Michael Casey)
Sermons for the Summer Season
Sermons on Conversion
Sermons on the Song of Songs I - IV
The Steps of Humility and Pride

THE WORKS OF WILLIAM OF SAINT THIERRY

The Enigma of Faith
Exposition on the Epistle to the Romans
Exposition on the Song of Songs
The Golden Epistle
The Mirror of Faith
The Nature of Dignity of Love
On Contemplating God, Prayer & Meditations

THE WORKS OF AELRED OF RIEVAULX

Dialogue on the Soul
Liturgical Sermons, I
The Mirror of Charity
Spiritual Friendship
Treatises I: On Jesus at the Age of Twelve, Rule for a
Recluse, The Pastoral Prayer
Walter Daniel: The Life of Aelred of Rievaulx

THE WORKS OF JOHN OF FORD

Sermons on the Final Verses of the Songs of Songs
I - VII

THE WORKS OF GILBERT OF HOYLAND

Sermons on the Songs of Songs I-III
Treatises, Sermons and Epistles

OTHER EARLY CISTERCIAN WRITERS

The Letters of Adam of Perseigne I
Alan of Lille: The Art of Preaching
Baldwin of Ford: Spiritual Tractates I - II
Gertrud the Great of Helfta: Spiritual Exercises
Gertrud the Great of Helfta: The Herald of God's
Loving-Kindness
Guerric of Igny: Liturgical Sermons I -[II]
Idung of Prüfening: Cistercians and Cluniacs: The
Case of Cîteaux
Isaac of Stella: Sermons on the Christian Year,I - [II]
The Life of Beatrice of Nazareth
Serlo of Wilton & Serlo of Savigny: Works
Stephen of Lexington: Letters from Ireland
Stephen of Sawley: Treatises

—MONASTIC TEXTS—

EASTERN CHRISTIAN TRADITION

Besa: The Life of Shenoute
Cyril of Scythopolis: Lives of the Monks of Palestine
Dorotheos of Gaza: Discourses and Sayings
Evagrius Ponticus:Praktikos and Chapters on Prayer
Handmaids of the Lord: The Lives of Holy Women in
Late Antiquity & the Early Middle Ages
(Joan Petersen)
The Harlots of the Desert (Benedicta Ward)
John Moschos: The Spiritual Meadow
The Lives of the Desert Fathers
The Lives of Simeon Stylites (Robert Doran)
The Luminous Eye (Sebastian Brock)
Mena of Nikiou: Isaac of Alexandra & St Macrobius
Pachomian Koinonia I - III (Armand Vielleux)
Paphnutius: A Histories of the Monks of Upper Egypt
The Sayings of the Desert Fathers (B. Ward)
Spiritual Direction in the Early Christian East (Irénée
Hausherr)
Spiritually Beneficial Tales of Paul, Bishop of
Monembasia (John Wortley)
Symeon the New Theologian: The Theological and
Practical Treatises & The Three Theological
Discourses (P. McGuckin)
Theodoret of Cyrrhus: A History of the Monks of Syria
The Syriac Fathers on Prayer and the Spiritual Life
(Sebastian Brock)

WESTERN CHRISTIAN TRADITION

Anselm of Canterbury: Letters I - III (W. Fröhlich)
Bede: Commentary on the Acts of the Apostles
Bede: Commentary on the Seven Catholic Epistles
Bede: Homilies on the Gospels I - II
The Celtic Monk (U. O Maidin)
Gregory the Great: Forty Gospel Homilies
The Meditations of Guigo I, Prior of the Charterhouse
(A. Gordon Mursell)
Peter of Celle: Selected Works
The Letters of Armand-Jean de Rancé I - II
The Rule of the Master
The Rule of Saint Augustine
The Wound of Love: A Carthusian Miscellany

CHRISTIAN SPIRITUALITY

Abba: Guides to Wholeness & Holiness East & West
A Cloud of Witnesses: The Development of Christian
Doctrine (D.N. Bell)
The Call of Wild Geese (M. Kelty)
Cistercian Way (André Louf)
The Contemplative Path
Drinking From the Hidden Fountain (T. Spidlík)
Eros and Allegory: Medieval Exegesis of the Song of
Songs (Denys Turner)
Fathers Talking (Aelred Squire)
Friendship and Community (B. McGuire)
From Cloister to Classroom
The Silent Herald of Unity: The Life of Maria Gabrielle
Sagheddu (M. Driscoll)
Life of St Mary Magdalene and of Her Sister
St Martha (D. Mycoff)

Many Mansions (D. N. Bell)
The Name of Jesus (Irénée Hausherr)
No Moment Too Small (Norvene Vest)
Penthos: The Doctrine of Compunction in the
   Christian East (Irénée Hausherr)
Rancé and the Trappist Legacy (A.J. Krailsheimer)
The Roots of the Modern Christian Tradition
   Russian Mystics (S. Bolshakoff)
Sermons in A Monastery (M. Kelty)
The Spirituality of the Christian East (Tomas Spidlík)
The Spirituality of the Medieval West (André Vauchez)
Tuning In To Grace (André Louf)
Wholly Animals: A Book of Beastly Tales (D.N. Bell)

—MONASTIC STUDIES—

Community & Abbot in the Rule of St Benedict I - II
   (Adalbert De Vogüé)
The Finances of the Cistercian Order in the
   Fourteenth Century (Peter King)
Fountains Abbey & Its Benefactors (Joan Wardrop)
The Hermit Monks of Grandmont (Carole A.
   Hutchison)
In the Unity of the Holy Spirit (Sighard Kleiner)
The Joy of Learning & the Love of God: Essays in
   Honor of Jean Leclercq
Monastic Practices (Charles Cummings)
The Occupation of Celtic Sites in Ireland by the
   Canons Regular of St Augustine and the
   Cistercians (Geraldine Carville)
Reading Saint Benedict (Adalbert de Vogüé)
The Rule of St Benedict: A Doctrinal and Spiritual
   Commentary (Adalbert de Vogüé)
The Rule of St Benedict (Br. Pinocchio)
Serving God First (Sighard Kleiner)
St Hugh of Lincoln (D.H. Farmer)
Stones Laid Before the Lord (A. Dimier)
What Nuns Read (D. N. Bell)
With Greater Liberty: A Short History of Christian
   Monasticism & Religious Orders (K. Frank)

—CISTERCIAN STUDIES—

Aelred of Rievaulx: A Study (A. Squire)
Athirst for God: Spiritual Desire in Bernard of
   Clairvaux's Sermonson the the Song of Songs
   (M. Casey)
Beatrice of Nazareth in Her Context
   (Roger De Ganck)
Bernard of Clairvaux & the Cistercian Spirit
   (Jean Leclercq)
Bernard of Clairvaux: Man, Monk, Mystic
   (M. Casey) Tapes and readings
Bernard of Clairvaux: Studies Presented to Dom Jean
   Leclercq
Bernardus Magister (Nonacentenary)
Christ the Way: The Christology of Guerric of Igny
   (John Morson)
Cistercian Sign Language (R. Barakat)
The Cistercian Spirit
The Cistercians in Denmark (Brian McGuire)
The Cistercians in Scandinavia (James France)
A Difficult Saint (B. McGuire)

The Eleventh-century Background of Cîteaux
   (Bede K. Lackner)
A Gathering of Friends: Learning & Spirituality in John
   of Forde (Costello and Holdsworth)
Image and Likeness: The Augustinian Spirituality
   of William of St Thierry (D.N. Bell)
An Index of Authors & Works in Cistercian Libraries in
   Great Britain I (D.N. Bell)
The Mystical Theology of St Bernard (Etiénne Gilson)
Nicolas Cotheret's Annals of Cîteaux (Louis J. Lekai)
A Second Look at Saint Bernard (J.Leclercq)
The Spiritual Teachings of St Bernard of Clairvaux
   (J.R. Sommerfeldt)
Studiosorum Speculum [L. J. Lekai]
Towards Unification with God (Beatrice of Nazareth
   in Her Context, 2)
William, Abbot of St Thierry
Women and St Bernard of Clairvaux (Jean Leclercq)

—MEDIEVAL RELIGIOUS—
WOMEN
Lillian Thomas Shank and John A. Nichols, editors

Distant Echoes
Peace Weavers
Hidden Springs: Cistercian Monastic Women, 2 Vol.

—CARTHUSIAN TRADITION—

The Call of Silent Love
Guigo II: The Ladder of Monks & Twelve Meditations
   (Colledge & Walsh)
Meditations of Guigo II (A. G. Mursell)
The Way of Silent Love (A Carthusian Miscellany)
The Wound of Love (A Carthusian Miscellany)
They Speak by Silences (A Carthusian)

—STUDIES IN CISTERCIAN—
ART & ARCHITECTURE
Meredith Parsons Lillich, editor

Volumes II, III and IV are now available

—THOMAS MERTON—

The Climate of Monastic Prayer (T. Merton)
The Legacy of Thomas Merton (P. Hart)
The Message of Thomas Merton (P. Hart)
The Monastic Journey of Thomas Merton (P. Hart)
Thomas Merton Monk & Artist (V. Kramer)
Thomas Merton on St Bernard
Toward an Integrated Humanity (M. Basil
   Pennington ed.)

—CISTERCIAN LITURGICAL—
DOCUMENTS SERIES
Chrysogonus Waddell, ocso, editor

Hymn Collection of the Abbey of the Paracletee
Institutiones nostrae: The Paraclete Statutes
Molesme Summer-Season Breviary (4 volumes)
Old French Ordinary & Breviary of the Abbey of the
   Paraclete: Text & Commentary (2 volumes)